The Role Of Religion In Politics And Society

Edited by
Harold Heie
A. James Rudin
Marvin R. Wilson

Published by the
Center for Christian Studies of Gordon College
and the
Interreligious Affairs Department of the American Jewish Committee

For information on publishers, contact:
Center for Christian Studies
Gordon College
255 Grapevine Road
Wenham, MA 01984

Interreligious Affairs Department
The American Jewish Committee
165 East 56th Street
New York, NY 10022

For purchase of additional copies, contact the Center for Christian
Studies

ISBN 0-9663481-0-9

The symposium that led to the publication of this book was made
possible in part through a grant from Leonard and Phyllis
Greenberg of Boyton Beach, Florida.

Book Design by George Payne

Book Editing by Amy Kvistad

CONTENTS

Page

Foreword: R. Judson Carlberg   7

Introduction: Issues at the Interface of Religion and Politics   15
Harold Heie

I.   Do Religion and Politics Mix?

Mixing Religion and Politics: A Separationist View   33
Barry W. Lynn

Do Politics and Religion Mix?   47
Janet Parshall

II.   Alternative Views of Pluralism: Christian Perspectives

Pluralism as a Matter of Principle   63
James W. Skillen

Pluralism: Another Word for Freedom   69
James M. Dunn

III.   Alternative Views of Pluralism: Jewish Perspectives

God is Not a Pluralist   79
David Klinghoffer

A Jewish Perspective on the Religious Right   87
A. James Rudin

IV.   Prayer in the Public Schools

        Prayer and Related Matters in the Public Schools   99
        Samuel Rabinove

        Prayer in the Public Schools   107
        Craig L. Parshall

V.   Conclusion

        First Amendment Considerations and Concluding   115
        Remarks
        Carl H. Esbeck

        Reflections on Christians in the Political Process   131
        Thomas A. Askew

FOREWORD

R. Judson Carlberg

I came to the symposium on "The Role of Religion in Politics and Society" with some deeply held beliefs. As a Christian I wanted to support the position that faith does have a very important role to play in society today. The presenters and subsequent interchanges helped me to clarify what the nature of that role ought to be and why religion ought *not* to be linked with government.

What I thought might simply be a quiet discussion among academics and public opinion leaders suddenly turned to concrete reality—and I was in the middle. At the close of the opening session, held on the Gordon College campus, a reporter approached me with a simple, direct and pointed question: "Has Gordon College ever had a church-state issue arise where the government intruded into your institutional life?"

We were standing in the beautiful A. J. Gordon Memorial Chapel, opened in 1993. I looked up for a moment at the large cross high above the platform. The question brought back some interesting memories. As I told the reporter, shortly after the building was opened, the local high school principal called to ask if it could be used for the district's graduation ceremonies. Wanting to be a good member of our community, I agreed.

Several days later, after the graduation committee toured the facility, I received another call. "May we have your permission to hang our high school banner across the platform?" the principal asked. He went on to explain that hanging the banner had been a tradition, and the school wanted to continue it. Then came a troubling little addendum. "Oh, by the way," he said, "it's so large it'll obscure the cross."

I explained my dilemma to the reporter. If I said, "No, the banner cannot be hung," I would no doubt create a major problem for the committee and the community. The banner display is a real town tradition. And there was another issue involved. Our community is made up of people of many faiths. By requiring a cross to be in a dominant position during a publicly supported town event, we could be challenged for creating a church-state problem.

Then I noted a major concern on the campus side. Allowing the banner to be hung over the cross would offend some people within our community. Some might even construe it as an erosion of the meaning of our most important Christian symbol. I didn't want that for a moment.

As I told the reporter, I had a tinge of resentment that I was put on the spot. "If we're a Christian college," I recalled thinking, "couldn't we display the cross when a publicly supported high school uses our facilities."

The Outcome

Some eyebrows were raised by my decision to let the banner be hung. Did Gordon compromise its institutional identity and integrity? Were we capitulating to an unwarranted intrusion by the state? Did we shift the delicate balance between the rights of religious people and the rights of the state? Was this the place and the point to draw the line?

The symposium addressed these and a number of other questions inherent in the conversation with the reporter. How should

Christians respond to perceived government intrusion? When should we resist state intrusion? Can we be faithful to our deeply cherished beliefs, be good citizens in our community, yet not break the law? When is accommodation justified for the common good? On the other hand, should we as Christians or Jews insist that our government be more reflective of a Judeo-Christian perspective?

These are important questions which any organization with deep religious convictions must answer. The reporter asked how I reached my decision. Here are some guiding principles I used. Many of them were confirmed by the symposium on our campus.

Gordon College was not hindered in any way from carrying out its essential mission by allowing the banner to be hung. Our fundamental right to exercise our religious commitments wasn't abridged or eroded. If the state had challenged our mission—to prepare graduates of intellectual maturity and Christian character, committed to servanthood and prepared for leadership—then we would have drawn the line and resisted!

But if our mission was not eroded, then did our commitment to the larger community require a reciprocal sensitivity to people of other faiths? A school district is a tax supported, publicly operated institution. It consists of those from many faiths—or no faith. I reasoned that high school graduates *should not be required* to attend a publicly supported ceremony in a building adorned by significant religious symbols of any faith.

Upon further reflection, I concluded that our chapel actually has many uses—some religious, many not. It certainly is not exclusively a place of formal worship. The building is used as a performing arts center, a concert hall, a theater and even a venue for lectures. Most of the time, the cross stands unobscured. But the building is also rented to outside groups for a multitude of purposes. Within reason, we allow changes to be made in the appearance and arrangements of the building to accommodate these users. Religious symbols are not necessarily appropriate in all of these circumstances. So use and users may determine when religious symbols are appropriate in a multi-use building.

In the case of the high school graduation, the school board did not attempt to influence or control what we taught in the chapel, our classes or in our residence halls. If there had been any pressure of that sort, we would have been on solid ground to refuse the use of the facility. The government should neither endorse nor limit what we do in our educational offerings.

By the same token, Christians should not enter into alliances with the government which could be construed as granting favor to one particular religion. The state must avoid any appearance of coercion when religion is involved. The concept of the separation of church and state is deeply ingrained in the founding principles of our government and nation. Many court decisions have affirmed this avoidance of coercion.

I also recognized that several very significant Christian faith traditions were built in part on the need to erect high walls between churches and civil government. This separation concept is still vitally important to a wide range of Christians. It is an important element in Baptist belief and is deeply ingrained in our college's history. Since I am from that tradition, I understand this issue well. In fact, I feel uneasy about many manifestations of the meaningless civil religion which remain a part of American public life.

A Response

How should Christians and observant Jews respond? Should we cooperate with those who would like to see religion torn from public life? Of course not. There are many times when it is appropriate for religious views to enter the public square. Religious peo-

10

ple should not be silent on crucial issues involving moral choices or ethical decisions. We have every right to be heard. The First Amendment right to free speech cuts both ways.

I concur with many in our country who maintain that our culture is in crisis. Judeo-Christian values are being eroded. The fabric of our society is crumbling. But I doubt that having religious symbols at state-sponsored events will help to turn the tide. This isn't the place to lay down the challenge. As Irving Krisol wryly observed in a *Wall Street Journal* opinion piece on this theme "...It is a well-known scientific fact that singing traditional Christmas carols doesn't even convert Christians to Christianity" (WSJ 12/22/95).

Religiously committed people can and should be evident in the public square. Gordon College exists to prepare men and women to practice their Christianity in a public and open manner—to influence public debate, uphold Judeo-Christian values, make wise and ethical choices and hold others in leadership roles to a higher standard of accountability. Jewish institutions of higher education rightly assert their responsibility to prepare their graduates to influence society from a value base built on Jewish religion, culture and history.

As President Clinton has said, "The First Amendment to the Constitution guarantees the freedom of religion—not the freedom from religion." The nonreligious world is beginning to understand this important distinction.

Let's acknowledge up front that there are cases where the state has become intrusive and restrictive in religious affairs. Mistakes have been made by public officials. When these occur, protectors of religious traditions must respond by bringing to bear the best legal arguments which support their position. And let's remember too that intrusion hasn't always been anti-religious. There are cases

11

where zealous government officials have favored Christianity above all else. And in today's litigious environment these cases usually end up in court.

For example, for years the high school in North Pontotoc, Mississippi allowed the school day to begin with students reading from the Bible and reciting prayers over the intercom. The school's curriculum included a course in Bible history, which critics maintained was an extension of a Sunday School class. One family has now filed suit to block this activity, and the case is slowly moving through the courts and gaining national prominence.

The legal system is available to seek corrective action for both sides in this debate. Private centers exist to monitor errors in judgment by public officials intruding into religious matters beyond their domain. Suits are frequently brought to protect religious rights. The court system is hearing those suits. Indeed, in several notable cases recently, it has affirmed the right of individuals to practice their religious beliefs unfettered by state interference.

Let's not confuse the practice of religion by individuals and groups with the establishment of religion by the state. The First Amendment to the Constitution guarantees Americans the right to practice religion. It also prohibits the state from establishing a particular religion.

When individual or corporate rights to worship are trampled upon, we must resist. We must continue to remember that "We, the people," have controlling interest in the government. "We, the people," can exercise our rights to speak out against and remove those who would erode things we believe in.

By the same logic we should be willing to avoid any coercive action which might violate the principle which prohibits state sanction of religion. Care must be exercised when challenging the so-called "leftist establishment" or the "Religious Right." Too many shrill voices on both sides are causing polarization within our country today. We must seek ground where dialogue can transpire, where civility is protected, where control and coercion are avoided.

In a pluralistic society Christians and Jews must insist on their right to be heard. We cannot allow every other group a platform in the public square while a muzzle is kept on people of faith. Separation of church and state does not mean the religious perspective is no longer valid or has lost its vitality.

Did I make the right decision on the banner and the cross? As I reflect on the perspectives contained in this book, I think so. But the symposium forced me to deal with the fact that these issues are far more complicated and call for far deeper reflection than I've usually encountered on either side. For that new insight, despite my anguish at the time, I'm grateful.

INTRODUCTION

ISSUES AT THE INTERFACE OF RELIGION AND POLITICS

Harold Heie

One doesn't have to look far in this conflict-torn world for evidence that it is difficult to initiate and sustain conversation about our deeply rooted disagreements concerning politics and religion, and their interface. From Bosnia to Northern Ireland to the West Bank, the evidence suggests that we are more inclined to violence than to conversation over our disagreements. And the events surrounding the horror of the courthouse bombing in Oklahoma City suggest that this tendency lies closer to home than many of us are willing to admit.

Against this backdrop, the purpose of this volume is to report on a conversation; one between Christian and Jewish scholars and leaders on various themes related to "The Role of Religion in Politics and Society." We didn't just expect disagreements, we orchestrated them by inviting speakers on each theme whom we knew to disagree with each other. This reflects our conviction that the growing contemporary debate about the appropriate role of religious communities in politics is not well served by the polemics of radio and TV talk shows, where those who disagree are often ridiculed and belittled, rather than engaged in conversation. Our ideal is for people who disagree with each other to talk, so that we can better understand each other's positions, and learn from each other. To do that, the disagreements have to first get out on the table.

That our symposium participants did in fact disagree with each other will soon be evident to the reader. The purpose of this introductory chapter is to attempt to identify some issues that appeared to lie at the root of these various disagreements. The identification of these issues will often be accompanied by questions that we encourage you, the reader, to struggle with as you attempt to develop your own informed beliefs about these pivotal issues.

An undeniable empirical fact that informs this conversation is that the American mosaic contains a plurality of expressions of religious commitment. Hence, the problem this fact raises is that of determining how this religious pluralism should, or should not, inform our attempts to govern ourselves politically. This suggests a first major foundational issue: What is the appropriate scope of expression of a person's religious commitment?

At one end of the spectrum on this issue are those who take the position that religious expression is essentially a private matter that should not impinge on the public square. Religious devotion may be expressed in private, or in the home or church or synagogue, or possibly in a close-knit neighborhood composed of persons of like faith. But such religious devotion should not spill over into public affairs.[1] This view appears to embrace a strict sacred/secular dichotomy.

---

[1] Stephen Carter refers to an extreme version of this view as akin to treating "Religion as a Hobby": The Culture of Disbelief: How American Law and Politics Trivialize Religious Devotion (New York: Basic Books, 1993), p. 29.

The symposium participant who appears closest to this view is David Klinghoffer, as he reflects on his own Jewish religious devotion. Although he doesn't directly address the issue of possible involvement of Jewish persons in the public arena, hints emerged from his comments in some of the symposium discussions. For example, he wouldn't argue for the inclusion of Jewish perspectives in public school education, because Jewish children shouldn't be in public school. Furthermore, his understanding of the Jewish religion is that it does not call for proselytizing (contrary to "an innovative view that has been taken recently by some Reform rabbis"). This suggests at least a hesitancy to bring Jewish perspectives to bear on public discussions with those of other religious faiths.

These hints point toward a need for Jewish apolitical separateness, and Klinghoffer does present some powerful and poignant reasons for such a view, reasons that non-Jewish persons may never fully appreciate. Separateness may be required to insure the very survival of Judaism. The Jewish people are still a people in exile. And the attempt to assimilate Jewish people into American culture is producing "Jews who have forgotten that they are Jewish." Klinghoffer suggests that "you modern-day Christian Americans kill us with kindness."

It is important to note the theological/philosophical basis for the Jewish separateness that Klinghoffer argues for (as if the need for survival were not sufficient). He asks the crucial question as to whether "Religion is about man, or (whether) it is about God?" He asserts that "if religion is about man, if it is man's creation, then we are correct to celebrate religious difference." Religious pluralism is then appropriate. But, "if religion is about God, and about truth, I'm afraid the situation is different. If God cares about the truth, about what we believe to be the truth—and that is the assumption of Western religion, whether Jewish or Christian, then we are obliged to act and speak accordingly." Klinghoffer concludes that

"God...is not...a pluralist," and, by inference, neither should we be, whether we are Christian or Jewish.

Klinghoffer's position raises a very important sub-issue, one that is noted by Carl Esbeck later in the symposium. Is a certain degree of separateness from the prevailing culture necessary for the survival of any religion? Esbeck suggests that only "thick religions" that "strongly resist being diluted...are the ones with staying power; acculturated religions are so 'thinned out' that they will suffer assimilation."[2]

At the other end of the spectrum from Klinghoffer on the first issue of the appropriate scope of expression of a person's religious commitment is the view that one's religious commitment encompasses all of life, and should therefore be expressed in the public square, not only in the privacy of one's home, church or synagogue, or immediate neighborhood. This view rejects a sacred/secular dualism. This appears to be the view advocated by Jim Skillen, and, as Skillen notes, the crucial political and constitutional question implicit in this view is "whether citizens are free to live according to their convictions outside as well as inside their churches and synagogues."

Skillen's concern is to protect the prerogatives of mediating structures, like the family and the church or synagogue, from government intrusion. However, based on the Reformed Christian perspective that orients Skillen's argument, Christians should still bring their religious convictions to the public debate regarding matters that fall within the proper scope of governmental responsibili-

---

2 For a helpful analysis of the distinction between "thick" and "thin" viewpoints, applied to moral discourse, see Michael Walzer, Thick and Thin: Moral Argument at Home and Abroad (Notre Dame, IN: University of Notre Dame Press, 1994).

ty, based on a foundational belief that Christians are called to be transforming agents in society.

It would appear, at first glance, that those symposium participants who are advocating a high wall of separation between church and state, such as Barry Lynn and James Dunn, are taking positions similar to Skillen by allowing for the fact that one's religious convictions unavoidably inform one's politics. As Barry Lynn states it: "Nobody expects a politician with religious beliefs to hang them up before he or she walks into the Capitol rotunda or the Oval office." Or, in the words of James Dunn, "Separation of church and state does not mean...separation of politics from religion." However, the appearance of similarity to Skillen's view is illusory. It is true that all three would argue for the legitimacy of expressing one's religious convictions in the public square. But I believe Skillen has a broader view of religion encompassing all of life than does Lynn or Dunn, and this leads Skillen to adopt a more qualified view of the proper scope of politics than I believe either Lynn or Dunn would take.

This brings us to our second major foundational issue: What is the proper scope of politics? One would expect there to be an inverse relationship relative to these first two issues; with a broad view of the scope of religion corresponding to a narrow view of the scope of government. A concrete example may help to clarify both of these issues, as well as the differences between Skillen and Lynn/Dunn.

Consider the issue of public financial support for education provided under religious auspices. Those persons situated toward the "private religion" end of the spectrum on the first issue of the proper scope of religion would typically oppose such support, as would Lynn and Dunn, arguing that this violates their understanding of the First Amendment and that it is the appropriate role of the government to offer free "secular" education to all young people.

Parents who want some other kind of education for their children should be allowed to pay for private education, in addition to their normal public school taxes. However, even those parents could, and should, bring their religiously informed beliefs to the school board meeting that discusses the curriculum for a given public school system. For example, they are free to propose, on religious grounds, that there should be more structures that provide for greater individual interaction between teacher and students because the teacher/student relationship, like all human relationships, should be a deeply caring relationship, because that is how Jesus taught us to relate to people. Other parents at the meeting, arguing from different religious or other worldview commitments may reach the same conclusion for different reasons, or may reach different conclusions. This public debate, informed by differing religious commitments, would be legitimate, for both Lynn and Dunn, as long as the outcome for school policy did not entail any particular "religious" input into the classroom.

On the other hand, what can be conjectured about those parents who situate themselves toward the other end of the spectrum on the first issue of the appropriate scope of religion—those who take the broad view that one's religious convictions ought to inform all of life? In a meeting of a school board for a public school system, they could and should, likewise, bring their religiously informed beliefs to the discussion of curriculum. But, they would also have a concern about the prior assumption that it is the appropriate role of government to educate all, or most, young people. They would argue, as does Skillen, but not Lynn or Dunn, on the basis of a broad view of the proper scope of religion, that it is a parental responsibility to decide on the type of education their children should receive, congruent with their religious convictions, thereby limiting the scope of government in providing education. They would further argue that the appropriate task of government is to treat all citizens fairly, and, therefore, government should not burden those who choose education under intentional religious auspices with "paying twice." According to this view, just and fair education policy would be to provide public support for a diversity of parentally chosen schools, whether "religious" or "secular," thus opening up more public space to religious expression.

But this view raises an important question. If we move away from the "common public school" concept, isn't there the danger of further fragmentation within our society? Some participants voiced this concern. On the other hand, in one of the discussion sessions, William Harper suggested that in certain European countries the practice of giving more choices to mediating groups situated between individuals and government has created a stronger allegiance to the nations that made that possible. Therefore, Harper conjectures that "if we pluralize in the right way, we can find the basis of the unity we are so desperately seeking."

The point of this extended example is not to take sides on these first two issues, though I have sides to take. Rather it is to illustrate that one's position on the first issue of the proper scope of religion may have a dramatic effect on one's position regarding the second issue of the proper scope of government.

However, unless you take the "strictly private religion" or "separatist religion" positions, whatever position you take on these first two issues would allow for some appropriate degree of expression of your religious convictions in the public domain. This raises a third major issue: What is the appropriate "force" that you should exert in expressing your religious convictions in the public domain? How adamant should you be about your convictions? To what extent, if any, should you seek to "impose" your religious convictions on those in the public square who hold to different religious convictions? To what extent, if any, should you be willing to "temper" (some would say "compromise") the implications of your religious convictions in light of contrary implications of the religious convictions of others?[3]

I can discern three alternative positions that participants took on this issue, the first two of which suggest that the prior issue is whether you believe your religious convictions are "true," or not. The first position starts with the firm belief that my religious convictions are "true;" true not just for me and my particular faith community, but universally true for everyone. In brief, this first position is that if one does indeed possess "the truth," then every effort should be made to legislate that truth through the political process. To do anything less than that is to compromise one's convictions about "the truth." This position appears to inform the arguments presented by Janet Parshall and Craig Parshall for prayer in the public schools. A central argument appears to be that our nation's founding fathers often endorsed "public accommodation to prayer and religious practice." Their intent was not to prohibit prayer and other religious practice in the public square. Rather, their concern was that government not use its power to "compel 'anyone' to worship in any way contrary to the dictates of conscience." Based on this understanding of intent, Craig Parshall argues for the practice of "voluntary" prayer in the public schools.

Granted that there is much historical debate about the "intent" of the founding fathers, and much legal debate as to the extent to which intent, even if it can be ascertained, is central to contemporary constitutional interpretation, the point of Craig Parshall's argu-

---

[3] I am taking the position here that the world is not divided into two groups, the religious and the non-religious. I espouse a broad definition of religion as referring to any set of beliefs, attitudes and practices informed by a "world-view" as to the ultimate nature of reality and my place in that reality. Under this definition, each one of us is "religious," including the atheist.

ment is that if his account is "true," as he firmly believes it is, then that "truth" needs to be normative for all American citizens, and that "truth" allows for voluntary prayer in the public schools.

As was to be expected, Craig Parshall's arguments generated lively discussion. While Samuel Rabinove had no difficulty with a "directed moment of silence" in the public school classroom, during which a given student could choose to pray, or not, he argued that "the right to engage in voluntary prayer does not include the right to have a captive audience listen—or to coerce other students to participate." After all, genuine expressions of religious commitment cannot be coerced; they are to be freely chosen. Some participants wondered about the purpose of a voluntary prayer program. If it is to teach students about the diversity of religious expression in our country, is it possibly better to include such instruction directly in the public school curriculum rather than to get at it indirectly through a rotating "prayer for the day" (or "deity for a day") program? Carl Esbeck asks whether "school prayer is a surrogate for two larger issues." First, for some advocates, "the desire for school prayer persists because...it is a visible sign as to who is in charge." He suggests that "where this is the case, we have the old Christian triumphalism," which "is to be condemned." On the other hand, the issue of school prayer may persist "because it answers the questions: 'Are we a nation under God?' and, 'Are human rights God-given?'." Although Craig Parshall does not address Esbeck's question of larger issues directly, I conjecture that his response would be that the "truth" of the matter is that America was founded as a "Nation under God," and that it is this "truth" that should compel Christians to express a strong political voice on behalf of voluntary prayer in the public schools.

Whereas this first position on the appropriate "force" of one's expression of religious convictions in the public domain assumes a strong view that one's convictions are universally "true," there is a second discernible position that starts with a more particularistic approach that allows for "multiple paths" to some ultimate "truth," whatever that is. The bare outlines of such a position were hinted at by James Rudin in the discussion following his paper.

Rudin noted that adherents to Judaism, Christianity or Islam are making "non-pluralistic, particularistic truth claims for themselves," but suggests that "they don't make too many claims of truth about the 'other'" (at least some Christians would disagree with that assertion). On that basis, Rudin suggests that religious thinkers need to develop a "theology of pluralism," and that such a theology might just allow for the possibility of "multiple paths to truth." In his own words, "is it possible...that after all of our strife and after all the problems for centuries between Christians and Jews and Muslims, that pluralism, diversity, and multiple paths to truth may in fact be the will of God?" Rudin's very choice of words reflects his own uncertainty about this possibility, but he encourages theologians to further explore its viability.

If one accepts the "multiple paths to truth" thesis, for the sake of argument, what are its implications for the appropriate "force" of one's expression of religious convictions in the public domain? Rudin provides a hint when he acknowledges the obvious religious diversity in our country, but notes that "we will have to work together on sewage and sanitation and water works and schools and the political realm and governance." He refers to this as a "de facto grudging kind of pluralism."

In a symposium discussion session, Wesley Roberts puts a more positive spin on Rudin's "grudging pluralism" by referring to a "functional pluralism." By this he means that "in order to function within the community and to do things that are good for the community, we have to come together and work and put our unique or special truth claims in the background in order to work."

Although Roberts' proposal may be functionally equivalent to Rudin's, in light of Rudin's concrete example regarding "sewage and sanitation...," there is an important difference that makes Roberts' proposal a discernible third position as to the appropriate "force" of one's expression of religious convictions in the public square. Whereas Rudin's philosophical/theological starting point holds to the possibility of "multiple paths to truth," Roberts' brackets the questions of the nature of ultimate truth or possible paths toward such truth.

Roberts' proposal suggests a strategy in the public square where we seek for "common ground" with adherents of differing religions on the concrete, specific issues that arise as we seek to live well together. This quest for common ground in a concrete situation does not require that we drive the discussion up (or, is it down?) to the more abstract level of universal truth claims about the overarching nature of reality. This means that as we engage in political discourse with others holding differing religious convictions, we do not dwell on the differing theological underpinnings that inform our attempts to address a concrete issue, such as how to deal with the problem of homelessness in our neighborhood. Rather, we seek common ground on the best practical way to deal with the concrete issue. Although we cannot find much common ground relative to our theological underpinnings, and we should not "force" that issue, hopefully we can find common ground on how to deal with some of the pressing human problems in our own backyards.

This proposed strategy of bracketing ultimate truth claims will surely raise the eyebrows of some who hold strong convictions that their truth claims are universal, applicable to all human beings, rather than particularistic, peculiar to the interpretive communities making such claims. But the practical reality is what Jonathan Sarna, in a discussion session, called the "plural superlative:" "I believe that my faith is best, but I do understand that there are other people who believe that their faith is best." There is little evidence that we can (or should?) reconcile our deep differences at the philosophical/theological level. And, besides, the pressing concrete problems that face our pluralistic communities cannot wait for any such supposed resolution.

But there may be more than a pragmatic reason for bracketing questions of ultimate truth in the public square. May I boldly suggest that there may be a good philosophical/theological reason that may be the kernel for the theology of pluralism that Rudin calls for. To get at this reason, I go back to some of the comments of David Klinghoffer.

I happen to agree with Klinghoffer that there is an ultimate truth known to God, and, therefore, God is not a pluralist relative to truth claims. But the fact is that I am not God, and I can't claim access to a "God's-eye view of truth." I must make a crucial distinction between the singular truth, as God knows it, and my limited partial glimpse of the nature of that truth. Because of that distinction, I must disagree with Klinghoffer's suggestion that "religion is about God and truth" and not "about man." Humans do not have unmediated access to God's truth. Therefore, I believe religion is "about God and man."

If I am right about this, then the starting point for a theology of pluralism may be the idea of epistemological humility, where I and others, holding to differing sets of ultimate truth claims, acknowledge that as finite, fallible human beings we may be wrong about some of our truth claims. That is hard to admit when you have strong convictions about your particular truth claims. But, Ian Barbour suggests that living well with that tension is a sign of religious maturity: "It is by no means easy to hold beliefs for which you would be willing to die, and yet remain open to new insights; but it is precisely such a combination of commitment and enquiry that constitutes religious maturity."[4]

If I and others in our pluralistic public square are characterized by such an attitude of humility about our ultimate truth claims, we may not feel so impelled to drive every discussion regarding concrete specific issues or problems up to arguments about our differing ultimate truth claims, thereby freeing us to seek some common ground relative to the issue at hand (fully recognizing that we may reach that common ground on the basis of differing philosophical/theological foundations).

Rudin's reference to a "grudging pluralism" and Roberts' proposal for a "functional pluralism" point to a related issue that clearly emerged at the symposium: What should we think about the very existence of pluralism? Is it a given to be tolerated and lived with as best we can? Or, is it a given that is to be celebrated? The center of gravity of opinion at the symposium appeared to lean toward toleration.

Klinghoffer acknowledges the existence of pluralism, but bemoans its consequences: "The consequences of pluralism are all around us: Jews who have forgotten they are Jewish." Although he refers to a "grudging pluralism," Rudin acknowledges a significant benefit of a properly ordered pluralism: "...it can be a protection or a shield against the worst that can happen to our groups as population minorities," noting, ironically, that therefore "Jews are pluralistic,...everywhere but in Israel." Roberts points to the necessity of a well ordered functional pluralism "because as human beings we need to live together and function together in spite of our religious differences." Carl Esbeck suggests that "religious and moral pluralism is not to be celebrated," or even "affirmed." Rather, "the first step is that pluralism should be acknowledged" and then be viewed

---

[4] Ian G. Barbour, <u>Myths, Models and Paradigms</u> (New York: Harper and Row, 1974), p. 136.

as "a formidable challenge: ...we should roll-up our sleeves and be about the hard task of making society work notwithstanding our deepest differences."

These are hardly voices of celebration. Jim Skillen strikes what is closest to a celebratory note when he suggests that the structural and confessional pluralism he argues for points to "pluralism as a matter of principle, not merely as a means of accommodating an unavoidable diversity." But I can't help but wonder whether we ought to be even more celebratory relative to the existence of diversity. Can't each of us be enriched by and learn from those who differ radically from us, even if our deep religious differences are irreconcilable? Once again, the answer to this question may have to do with humility.

The various positions that emerged at the symposium regarding the appropriate "force" of one's expression of religious convictions in the public square presuppose that there is openness in the public square to hearing "religious voices." Whether there is such openness is another major issue that emerged in the symposium. Janet Parshall sees no such openness. In fact, her perception is that there is "wide-spread hostility against religion in America's public institutions," and she cites a number of examples.

This issue raises the underlying thorny question as to the most appropriate interpretation of the First Amendment to the U.S. Constitution. Is the purpose of the First Amendment to eliminate all religious expression in the public square, thus opening the door to possible official "hostility" to religious public expression? Or, is it, rather, to avoid governmental coercion to adhere to any one particular religion and to avoid preferential treatment by government that favors any one particular religion? If it is the latter, as I am inclined to think, then there is no room for official hostility to voices in the public square informed by religious beliefs, as long as no religion is given preferential treatment.

28

Obviously, the issue of the most adequate interpretation of the First Amendment is for the Supreme Court to decide, not me, and there is no lack of conflicting opinion within the legal profession. For those of us outside the legal profession, the concluding essay by Carl Esbeck makes some very helpful distinctions. One that I found particularly helpful is the distinction between "government speech" and "private speech." If the purpose of the First Amendment is to circumscribe "government speech" regarding religion (as Esbeck seems to argue, quoting Justice O'Connor), then this does not preclude "private speech" by citizens that is informed by religious convictions, even within public institutions.

The above reflections are the result of one participant's attempt to identify some of the issues that appeared to lie at the root of the obvious disagreements that were expressed at this symposium. As you work your way through this book, you will no doubt be able to identify other pivotal issues. Hopefully, your reading of these essays will help you to formulate or clarify your own position on these varied issues.

Since this April 1995 symposium was the inaugural event for the Center for Christian Studies at Gordon College, which I direct, allow me to situate this symposium in the context of the primary mission of this Center. In brief, the major purpose of this Center is to foster scholarship informed by Christian perspectives and the dissemination of that scholarship to the larger academy and larger culture. An intentional strategy toward accomplishing this purpose will be the creation of "forums for conversation" that will enable Christian scholars to talk to other scholars, so that we can share the results of our respective scholarship and learn from each other. This strategy is based on our belief that in our increasingly con-tentious society, persons of good will who disagree strongly with each other can still learn from each other if they are willing to talk. From this participant's perspective, this symposium was a marvelous exemplification of this lofty ideal.

Of course, given the topic of conversation at this symposium, this conversation will never arrive at final answers, "good for all time" (as Carl Esbeck reminds us). Therefore, we need to keep talking.

There are many people who deserve much credit for the planning and implementation of this symposium. Foremost are the symposium co-chairpersons, Marvin Wilson, Harold John Ockenga Professor of Biblical Studies at Gordon College, and Rabbi A. James Rudin, Director of Interreligious Affairs of the American Jewish Committee. They have been involved in fruitful conversation about Christian/Jewish relations since 1975 and will continue such conversations long after this symposium.

A special word of thanks also goes to Rabbi Lori Forman, formerly of the American Jewish Committee, for her excellent collaboration in both planning and implementing this symposium. Thanks also to Debbie Chrysafidis of the Center for Christian Studies for her flawless handling of all the details of implementation.

Finally, thanks go to the "behind-the-scenes" staff members at Gordon College for their fine, unheralded work: Timothy Utton, Media Coordinator; Harry Durning, Director of Public Relations; Keith Harris, Director of Printing Services; Jack Lawrence, Director of Dining Services; Paul Helgesan, Director of Physical Plant; Ron Hilton, Director of Auxiliary Services; and Jeffrey Hoy, Director of Public Safety.

I. DO RELIGION AND POLITICS MIX?

MIXING RELIGION AND POLITICS: A SEPARATIONIST VIEW

Barry W. Lynn

Let me say at the outset that I don't know what Janet Parshall will say tonight. Since this is billed as "two different" views of the subject of religion and politics—it is obviously entirely up to her to come up with the different view. Since Janet and I have spent many hours debating on radio and television, though, I have this hunch she won't agree with either my premises or my suggested rules for mixing religion and politics. Just to make sure, I have of course escalated the level of inflammatory rhetoric just to be on the safe side.

Seriously, I do mention a number of people whom I would place generically on the "Christian Right," but I don't assume Janet necessarily agrees with all of their arguments, tactics, or analyses.

Let's get some of the "easy stuff" out of the way first. Nobody expects a politician with religious beliefs to hang them up before he or she walks into the Capitol rotunda or the Oval office. Similarly, this nation has a long, proud, continuing, Constitutionally-permitted, and ethically-appropriate tradition of religious leaders speaking a prophetic voice to their government, calling upon it to change when it is engaged in wrong-doing and praising it when it is on the correct moral path as those leaders see it. I certainly don't want to change either of those fundamental truths.

However there is a shadow on the landscape. It is a growing legion of religious leaders, organizations and movements (bolstered by self-interested political operatives) who would like to turn these United States into a theocracy, a government run along narrow sectarian lines: a government which is literally under their God, and where, *at best*, those who are not believers are tolerated.

For a period of two years I have been sitting at a microphone next to Pat Buchanan about three afternoons a week for a radio show on the Mutual Broadcasting System. And it was Pat who articulated at the 1992 Republican National Convention in Houston the sentiments of many in this movement. He announced, "We are in a religious war for the soul of America." I don't remember declaring this war—but all across America people are finding themselves reluctant draftees in a battle to determine if one religious group *will or will not gain* increased control over our lives and the lives of our children.

These groups and leaders are not compromisers, seeking some elusive common good. They are not interested in working this out together—they are intent on victory. When Pat Robertson's Christian Coalition comes each September to Washington, it is a "Road to Victory" conference. Last year's was "Road to Victory V." This year it will be "VI," surpassing even the number of <u>Rocky</u> sequels.

Just listen for a moment to the words of the people I am talking about: Here is Randall Terry, founder of Operation Rescue, in a Fort Wayne, Indiana paper in 1993:

> "I want you to just let a wave of intolerance wash over you. I want you to let a wave of hatred wash over you. Yes, hate is good. Our goal is a Christian nation. We have a biblical

duty. We are called on by God to conquer this country. We don't want equal time. We don't want pluralism."

And, here are Pat Robertson's views, articulated on his syndicated 700 Club in early 1991:

> "You say 'you're supposed to be nice to the Episcopalians and the Presbyterians and the Methodists and this, that, and the other thing.' Nonsense! I don't have to be nice to the spirit of the Anti-Christ."

If the Anti-Christ is represented by his fellow Protestant Christians, where in the world does that put everybody else—and who do *they* represent?

Frankly, with these declarations in the forefront, it is a tad unbelievable to hear representatives of Brother Robertson say that they and Pat have a deep commitment to an "inviolable" separation of church and state.

There are a few other assumptions which seem to undergird much of the debate about religion and politics. The first is that somehow religion has been ostracized from public life. Fr. Richard Neuhaus has characterized this phenomenon as the "naked public square." In fact, not only is the square not bare, it is not even clad in lingerie; it is fully clothed with all the vitality religion brings to our common life. By way of narrow rebuttal, I point out initially that virtually every religious group in the country has an office (most in Washington) dedicated to the communication of its views to government officials and to the public. Whenever there is even the perception of wrong-headedness about their faith, they clamor before the media to set it straight. All that Miramax Pictures had to do was announce it was opening the controversial film <u>Priest</u> in many cities on Good Friday, and the Catholic League for Civil and Religious Rights immediately issued a scathing denunciation of the company, and its parent organization the Walt Disney Company, because the film was allegedly blasphemous. On a much more significant and somber note, less than 24 hours after the horrific bombing in Oklahoma City, Muslim organizations in the United States were insisting (quite properly) that the news media and government officials be reticent to make assumptions that "Arabs" or "Islamic militants" were somehow involved.

Beyond Washington there is a veritable flood of voices in media outlets controlled by conservative religious groups. At recent gatherings of the Religious Broadcasters Association we learned that there are over 1,600 Christian radio stations, and 300 television stations in the country. Pat Robertson's 700 Club airs at least twice a day on the Family Channel, a basic cable service in virtually every metropolis, town, and hamlet in America. Psychologist/activist Dr. James Dobson holds forth on over 1,500 radio stations each day, and is capable of generating literally bagfuls of correspondence to Congress on any matter which strikes his fancy.

Lobbyists, broadcasters—these are not denizens of a world of darkness and silence at the bottom of the sea; they are integral to public debate and discussions, and America's religious community is a big contributor to all that.

The collateral claim to the "naked square" is that there is a "war against religion," particularly Christianity, in the popular culture. Now, if true, there must be a remarkably weak army allied against the faithful. Indeed, by every measure this is the most religious nation in the Western world. A higher percentage of Americans attend religious services, pray regularly, and say they believe in God than anywhere else, even in nations which have religion taxes or other official denominational support.

All the rhetoric, though, suggests that our official institutions evince hostility to religion. With that argument comes claims that the reason religious groups need to become more militantly political is to combat this strong opposition. The practical reality, though, is that people of faith are not living in an "alien nation." Our public schools, for example, are not the "value free" zones they are portrayed to be by politico-religious demogogues like Jerry Falwell and Pat Robertson who want to dismember the schools, and replace them with a web of sectarian private academies (at taxpayer expense). I went to my son's mid-year school night and came across posters all over the school promoting some shocking ideas. Can you believe it: Virginia schools taking this obviously left-wing, atheistic, Planned Parenthood-oriented, neo-satanic, probably Stalinist line of teaching: "honesty, respect, courtesy, fairness." Then my son's homeroom teacher has to go even beyond this: she has a list of "rights and responsibilities" containing such horrific propaganda as, "All students have a right to voice their opinion without being ridiculed."

Unfortunately, the entire universe of "values" often seems encompassed in schools by the Religious Right by a single question: "Do they give out condoms?" Everything else is unrecognizable as a moral statement. However, virtually every public school corridor has a poster communicating the message, "Don't Use Drugs." Some would be happier if it had a proof text from Genesis or Galatians but for many of us it is enough that the widely shared community value that crack is bad for children is a good enough statement, in and of itself, to justify its communication.

Every time a student is told to stop fighting in the hall or receives praise for doing well on an exam, he or she is the recepient of a transmitted value. No need to fear the absence of moral teaching in this most demonized of all public institutions; it is there.

In a nation where there is neither officially sanctioned animosity toward religion nor an absence of a strong voice for values in public policy debates, it is extremely important that religious groups conduct themselves in a manner consistent with constitutional principle and high ethical standards. Toward those ends, let me set out four ideas about the intersection of religion in political life.

First, we cannot allow what are, in essence, religious tests to be required for public office. Obviously, the Constitution itself prohibits such "tests" in a technical sense. The government cannot force a Congressional candidate or a presidential appointee to affirm allegiance to God. What we are seeing more of these days in Washington, though, are groups, in purpose and in result, requiring that at least certain government employees meet *their* theological standards. Obviously, this was clearest in the push to oppose the nomination of Dr. Henry Foster to serve as Surgeon General. Dr. Foster has a distinguished medical career, well in the mainstream of pediatric practice. He is fully capable of being a spokesperson for good health habits in this country. But within nanoseconds of the announcement of his nomination, he was being denounced by "right-of-center" groups like the Family Research Council, run by Gary Bauer, the Christian Coalition, and Ms. Parshall's former employer, Concerned Women for America. Dr. Foster's failing: he performed at least one abortion. His collateral crime: he was a member of the local Planned Parenthood board. As more scrutiny was given to the nomination, it appeared that Dr. Foster may have performed closer to 40 abortions.

You know what? For his critics, it doesn't matter how many he did. In fact, if he had not done any, but had merely told women where to get one from someone else, the same charges would be levied: "he cannot be Surgeon General, because he acts like the Supreme Court decision in *Roe vs. Wade* was right." In other words, he doesn't buy into the theological belief, and this is what it is, that human life exists and is deserving of full legal protection from the instant of conception. Therefore, he is *per se* disqualified.

Ralph Reed said that the Christian Coalition would be looking to see how Senator Bob Dole voted in regard to the Foster nomination. Funny thing, Senator Dole—then Presidential-candidate-who-would-love-the-votes-of-the-Christian-Coalition-members-Dole—announced on NBC that he might well block even Senate consideration of the nominee. Word does get around. Look carefully at the language of the Foster opposition: you find a test of political acceptability inextricably intertwined with a religious test.

Second, we must not countenance deceitful candidates for public office. Ralph Reed once said, in an interview I'm sure he has regretted more than once subsequently: "I like to do guerilla warfare. I paint my face. I travel by night. You don't know it's over until you wake up in a body bag." From this emerged the criticism of "stealth" candidates—candidates who will not disclose who they are or what they represent. They don't go to candidate forums; they don't answer questionaires from the League of Women Voters or the local newspaper. They campaign almost exclusively by having their campaign literature left under the windshield wiper blades at selected Christian church parking lots a few Sundays before election day.

Reed says they don't do that "stealth" stuff anymore. Well, they do—and worse. G. Gordon Liddy told the last Christian Coalition convention that they should behave more like the Communist Party—by placing secret "agents of influence" in important posts: "At the key moment they can cast a key vote and the other side doesn't know what's happened to them." Now this is real honesty and integrity coming from a well-known moral leader. (G. Gordon, of course, had briefly fallen from grace with the Religious Right after he asked female listeners to his daily radio show to send in photographs of themselves in their underwear carrying a gun, for a calendar he wanted to do. Apparently grace caught up with him quicky.) Liddy's strategy is still operative; it is

39

still wrong. At a minimum, the democratic process requires that candidates lay their cards on the table, honestly allowing voters to know what their positions are so they can make an informed choice. When you hide your political light under a bushel, you are slapping democracy in the face.

What happens when these "stealthers" get into office? Is it so bad? Sadly, the answer is "yes."

The Vista Unified School District in California was taken over by fundamentalist Christians in 1992. Within eight months, they had adopted policies—contrary to the recommendations of a panel of local science teachers it had established—to teach "creationism," and undercut generally established scientific theories of evolution. I asked the president of the school board one day on the radio if she would at least dissociate herself from some of the more extreme views of pro-creationist advocacy groups like the Institute for Creation Research. She asked, "Like what?" I said, "Specifically, should we teach that the reason the dinosaurs died was because they were too large to fit into Noah's ark?" She would not dissociate herself and countered with, "What are you afraid of if they learn that?" My response was very clear, "I'm afraid they will become scientific illiterates who will not be able to compete in the world of the 21st century." Most of those folks in Vista have now been removed from office by the electoral process. When the extremism of their views was exposed, it turned out to be time for them to go.

More good news. I don't know about you, but I was relieved that in a Republican primary in Lake County, Florida, three school board candidates were defeated in large measure because they had supported a school board resolution declaring that teachers had to teach that Western culture is inherently superior to all other "foreign and historic" ones on the planet. I say I was relieved for two reasons. First, I don't think education is about simply stating such generalities as truths and then insisting that people believe it.

Education is helping people understand how to judge differences and evaluate alternatives in order to reach a final decision about what is "superior." Then, second, I didn't really understand what the resolution meant. But, it is at least reassuring that I didn't even have to think that American cultural expressions like "Beavis and Butthead" or "Bowling for Dollars" are inherently superior art forms compared to, say, the Sistine Chapel or the Taj Mahal.

If you're going to take these extremist positions, let the voters learn before the election—and I am confident that in most communities this nonsense will not occur, not even for one election cycle.

On a similar note, we've been getting very disturbing reports for the past year about misrepresentations on "voting records" of candidates. For example, Indiana Congressman Andy Jacobs was characterized on the Indiana Chrisitian Coalition "voters guide" as an opponent of the balanced budget amendment. In fact, like it or not, he was one of the Democrats who created the thing. Perhaps lying is a biblical virtue, and I slept though my seminary class that morning. It is possible that Oliver North (roundly endorsed by Pat Robertson) may have attended in my place.

Third, there is an incredible arrogance on the part of some Christian advocacy groups. Pat Robertson calls his political arm "The" Christian Coalition, not a Christian coalition. This arrogates to one group the claim of morality for all Christians. Well, count me out. During the recent "great" debate on health care, Ralph Reed noted his opposition to inclusion of drug rehabilitation and mental illness coverage with the sweeping statement that "church-going families are less prone to use these programs, services they don't want or need." For some of us this sounds a little inconsistent with Jesus' answer to the man who asked, "When did we see you naked and clothe you? When did we see you hungry and feed you?" and Jesus replied, "When you did this for the least among you, you did it for me."

41

But when you have the arrogance of being able to know what "the" Christian position is, and when you know that this is a "Christian nation" (as so many on the right proclaim), there is little to do but find a "proof-text" in your Holy Scripture and apply it to solve—without debate—every issue.

A reporter called me to get my views about a comment she had received from a Congressman about why he voted not to cap the family tax credit at $95,000, but to extend it to families making $200,000. He told her the Gospel parable of the "talents," where Jesus criticized someone who had not invested money given to him, but had hidden it away to protect it. There is a certain logic to the analogy I suppose; at least more than to the claim of the now-defunct "Christian Voice" group that found direct scriptural support for both the abolition of the Department of Education and construction of the B-1 bomber.

Now, did that Congressman do something "unconstitutional" by referring to the parable? No. Did he do something "unconstitutional" even if that was the sole basis for his vote? Again, no. However, I think it is useful to suggest that if the parable is either an "excuse" to justify his vote or was the sole basis for his vote, there is perhaps an analytical insufficiency in his policy making. This is not because the values contained in the lessons of Scripture are not worthy of being taken seriously, but because Scripture is not the statute book of the United States. The "Contract with America" that guides this country is the Constitution.

Fourth, consider an extraordinary lawsuit that was filed in Washington, D.C. by the American Center for Law & Justice, Pat Robertson's legal arm. Let me just give you a little history.

In November of 1992, just four days before the presidential election, an ad appeared in USA Today. This $41,000 epistle read "Christian Beware" at the top, and then went on to argue that because Bill Clinton supported abortion rights, gay rights, and distribution of condoms in school, he was a sinner. The ad continued that a Christian who voted for a sinner became one him-or herself. These theological pronouncements were, appropriately, accompanied by "proof texts," specific references to biblical passages. At the bottom of the page, it noted in small print that the ad was paid for by the Church of Pierce Creek, a church located near Binghamton, New York, which, I subsequently learned was, among other things, the church of Operation Rescue founder Randall Terry. As it happened, I was in New Hampshire that morning and my wife read the paper first. She got to this, passed it over to me, and said, "Isn't this illegal?" When I read it, my reaction was, "Of course." Here was a church, tax exempt automatically under the internal revenue code, calling for the defeat of a specific candidate: electioneering. The tax code specifically prohibits any tax exempt organization, including churches, from participating in political campaigns, including support for or opposition to a candidate for public office. Americans United immediately filed a formal complaint with the IRS.

Within two weeks, the Internal Revenue Service had begun to move on the matter, questioning the church about the incident. After a series of meetings and written inquiries—and less than satisfactory answers from the church—the IRS indicated in a letter in January of 1995 that the church had lost its tax-exempt status.

In April of 1995, the ACLJ lead attorney Jay Sekulow held a press conference to announce that a lawsuit was being filed against the IRS alleging that they had no right to regulate what he called the "free speech" of churches. Not only does this complaint say that the tax code doesn't in fact prohibit churches from engaging in partisan politics, but it goes on to allege that the Constitution prohibits the government from ever doing so.

This argument is legally preposterous and ethically bankrupt.

If the tax agency has no authority to limit political activity, religious institutions in America will become the functional equivalent of utterly unregulated political action committees. A pastor could dump the contents of the collection plate into an envelope for Senate candidate Jones or School Board hopeful Smith, and no one dare complain about it. It is shocking to think that instead of the smell of incense in the sanctuary, we'll begin to smell the acrid cigar smoke of a political back room.

This case is not about one advertisement. It is about a fundamental shift in the role of churches in the political process. It is no coincidence that it was Pat Robertson's legal group which filed this suit, because Brother Robertson has the most to gain from a victory. For years, he has been luring churches into increasing political activity by trying to locate or place at least one Christian Coalition activist in each church. Many pastors who might fear the legal consequences of too heavy a political program would have no fear if the ACLJ's legal program prevails—or if adopted by Congress (the more likely approach).

The radical Religious Right talks democracy—it wants theocracy. It is ignorant or contemptuous, or both, of our Constitution and our history. Its leaders call separation of church and state a "lie of the left," yet they ignore the facts. George Washington wrote that this country was "in no way founded as a Christian nation." Thomas Jefferson wouldn't even declare days of thanksgiving. James Madison thought that the 1790 census would be unconstitutional if it contained a question asking whether you were a member of the clergy. These would be characterized as radical left sentiments today; yet they were the very ideas of the people who built America's political foundation.

We have an even bigger job ahead of us to stop the radical Religious Right from gaining more political control—and the achievement of their sectarian, extremist agenda. This isn't some intellectual chess game we're playing with them; the stakes, I believe are whether our children will live in a world of truth or lies, of embracing diversity or proclaiming bigotry, and of moving ahead with social progress or regressing to a new dark age.

DO POLITICS AND RELIGION MIX?

Janet Parshall

Our task, as I understand it, in this keynote address, is to present contrasting views on the question of whether politics and religion mix. Restating the question, we might ask it this way: to what extent should religion be brought to bear on the public policies of American government? This might appear to be quite a formidable question to answer. And in the two days of this symposium, even with the array of notable authorities who will be addressing this issue, it might be somewhat radical of me to suggest that the answer will be definitively presented. But there is one aspect of the relationship between religion and politics that is even more shocking than the thought of presenting an easy answer to this complex question; and that was the "shocking" suggestion contained in a political cartoon I saw once.

In the cartoon, two members of Congress were leaving their offices on Capitol Hill, with rather somber looks on their faces. One was saying to the other: "Mark my words, once we put prayer and Bible reading back in the schools, the next thing you know they will be expecting us to actually live by the ten commandments!" Now there is a radical thought!

Of course its easy to poke fun at the "Capitol Gang" when it comes to questions of morality or religion; but the fact is that I know quite a number of honest and conscientious Senators and members of Congress who are grappling with the fall-out of this question of the role of religion in the American public debate.

Perhaps more than any other single event, a speech given at the Heritage Foundation by Speaker of the House Newt Gingrich on October 5, 1994 acted as a catalyst for the debate that has been smoldering in the American political scene for some time. Here is some of what he said:

> "To my Democratic friends who believe that religious faith is archaic I would suggest to them that Franklin Roosevelt understood the world very, very well indeed and that, just as he opposed permanent welfare, he also opposed anti-religious, secular behaviors as being just plain stupid, because they are destructive to human beings. They weaken and cripple people. If you eliminate the soul, you probably also eliminate the person's capacity to live a decent life.

> So, from the standpoint of all of American history, if you want to understand us as a civilization, you have to begin with an understanding of the framework in which we were founded as a country. If you want to understand the founding fathers, I believe it is literally impossible to suggest that the founding fathers were engaged in a process by which they intended to have people live in a secular world. I think that you cannot historically prove that."

Gingrich went on to quote from de Tocqueville, that French observer of the early American experiment in the first 50 years of constitutional rule in America, who said: "Religion...must be regarded as the first of [the American] political institutions." That certainly gives one kind of answer to the question of whether religion and politics mix.

The terminology of the "mix" between religion and politics is interesting. I would suggest that there are three kinds of "mixes" in the physical world that perhaps can be used to make a point about the issues that we are talking about today.

First, there are those things that by their very nature are not capable of being mixed very well. Take water and gasoline as an example. They tend to separate naturally. We don't really have to exert a lot of oversight to keep them divided, because they do that on their own.

Then take, as a second example, fire and gasoline. There is nothing in their nature that is necessarily separate, yet we want to exercise the greatest caution to keep them away from each other because the combination, the "mix", could be disastrous. And when we do bring them together, in the combustion engine as an example, it is highly controlled. These are the dangerous "mixes."

And then thirdly, we have things that can be mixed, and they are not necessarily dangerous in themselves when combined—fire and water as an example. These two produce steam, the last time I checked. And when James Watt, in the 18th century, refined that combination into the steam engine it revolutionized industry. So there we have a "mix" that had profoundly creative and productive possibilities, and a low range of risk, particularly when compared with our second example.

As you may have guessed, I consider the interaction between religion and politics, on the whole, to be more like our third example. Certainly enough, the meeting of theological belief and public policy may (and often does) generate some heat and steam, but in that energy there is something productive that can be created. What this "mix" does not forbode is the kind of explosive and catastrophic scenario painted by the strict separationists.

Why do I say that a scenario of death and destruction has been painted by those who oppose an increased role of religion in American public life? First, take a look at the wide-spread hostility against religion in America's public institutions.

In Decatur, Illinois a primary school teacher discovered the word "God" in a phonics textbook and told her class to strike it out, telling the seven year olds that it was illegal to refer to God in a public school.

In the town of Oak Park, Illinois local officials prohibited a local private Catholic hospital from placing a cross on its own smokestack because some of the town residents might be offended.

A student recently was banned from going through with a planned mural he was going to paint. The problem apparently arose when officials of James Madison University discovered his theme: art major David Chang was planning on painting a replica of Michelangelo's "The Creation of Adam," on the wall of the dormitory lounge. According to Chang, the university official who vetoed the mural said the picture of God stretching out his hand to touch the lifeless form of Adam had the potential of being religiously offensive to someone.

And then there is eleven year old Andrew Hannas, an elementary student in public school in Chesapeake, Virginia. School administrators told him he could not read his Christmas holiday poem at the school's "Winter Festival." His self-created poem was a take-off on Clement Moore's famous 1823 "A Visit From St. Nicholas." Andrew's poem, which urged help for the homeless and the hungry and the necessity of instilling the values of avoiding drugs and violence, also made explicit reference to God and Jesus. Published accounts quote school spokesman Tom Cupitt as explaining: "We try to be fair to everybody. Schools are secular...we try to teach kids diversity."

I think it is worth quoting the last few lines of Andrew's banned poem. It reads:

> "So listen my children and you shall hear
> By God's word He is very near

So lend out your heart and not just your hand
Let Christmas live every day with peace throughout the
land."

What Andrew didn't know then, but he is probably starting to grasp now, is that there is no peace in the land when it comes to public mention of God in public institutions. There is indeed a culture war over the suitability of religious values in the secularized market place. And granted, in some of these acts of censorship of the faithful, government officials may be able to present administrative explanations to justify their actions. But the point is not whether the religious among us can always sustain the legal burden of proof in a court case. The point is that there is a prevailing tide of hostility, of official discrimination against the theist, particularly the biblical theist, and in many cases most especially the biblical theist with a conservative view of politics.

What we have is the "fire meets gasoline" view of the role of religion in our public places, which is to say it is to have as little a role as possible. Many excuses are available: a high regard for diversity and pluralism; a pure desire to avoid giving offence. But none of these ring true. The kind of strict separation of religion out of the public place in government and public institutions rivals, if not exceeds, the way we treat the real social evils among us, like race discrimination and child pornography. The only difference is that when religion is suppressed our government officials usually don't tell us that our religious symbols and practices are innately dangerous to the prevailing social order, they simply treat them as if they were.

And there is also the demonizing of religious values by the secular media, and the academic elite. What kind of image is created, as an example, in a cover story in the usually straight-talking/moderately conservative US News & World Report when they

51

almost singly identify the Christian conservative movement with Pat Robertson, and the "millions of foot soldiers, [and] full collection plates...?" The article, in a side-bar, reminds us that "evangelicals are less educated than the public but making strong gains." All of this harkens us back to the oft-condemned, but almost too bigoted-to-believe statement of the <u>Washington Post</u>, that Christian conservatives are poor, uneducated, and easy to command.

Or we can point to the January 1995 issue of <u>Cosmopolitan</u> magazine, which headlined its article on religion in politics with this huge banner: "THE FIERCE, FURIOUS MARCH OF THE FUNDAMENTALISTS." The bold-lettered caption on the next page was even more revealing where it tells the reader: "They're militantly anti-abortion...they believe feminism encourages women to practice witchcraft. And they're seizing political control in frightening numbers. (Being aware of what they're up to is crucial.)"

These are the caricatures of religion mixing with politics, the grotesque and misshapen images that would tell us that America is about to toss a match onto a sea of political gasoline. In law school they taught my husband "Caveat Emptor"—let the buyer beware. But I say: let the reading and listening public beware; let the citizenry of America beware. These grotesques are the shadowy imaginings of those who embrace the secular and fear the sacred.

This is not to ignore the real evils that can result from unholy alliances between religion and state. One of them was penned by Mao Tse-Tung in 1966 when he wrote: "Our God is none other than the masses of the Chinese people." Religion was, to him, something to be strangled by the state and replaced by totally secular ideals.

Another evil would be presented by laws that require citizens to perform religious acts or profess religious beliefs as a condition of some civil right. But is there anyone among us who would not recognize those kinds of threats? And do the mainstream of religious believers who are politically active really believe that those kinds of laws are appropriate? In short, there is a mile of territory between a democracy accommodating the religions of its people, and government by theocracy. And I believe the great majority of Americans can tell the difference even if the <u>Washington Post</u> cannot.

The dangers of official hostility toward religion, coupled with the selective demonizing of conservative religious views can lead to even more disturbing possibilities. Decades ago, C. S. Lewis wrote of the scenario where our new scientific and antireligious culture hides a real type of tyranny under the cloak of a "humanitarian" treatment for unpopular and politically incorrect beliefs. Lewis writes:

> "Of all tyrannies a tyranny sincerely exercised for the good of its victims may be the most oppressive...The robber baron's cruelty may sometimes sleep...but those who torment us for our own good will torment us without end for they do so with the approval of their own conscience...In reality, however, we must face the possibility of rulers armed with a humanitarian theory of punishment...We know that one school of psychology already regards religion as a neurosis. When this particular neurosis becomes inconvenient to government, what is to hinder government from proceeding to "cure" it? Such "cure" will, of course, be compulsory; but under the humanitarian theory it will not be called by the shocking name of persecution...The new Nero will approach us with the silky manners of a doctor...."[1]

---

[1] C.S. Lewis, The Humanitarian Theory of Punishment", <u>God In The Docks: Essays On Theology And Ethics</u> (Grand Rapids, MI: William B. Erdmans, 1970), pp.292, 293

This, of course, could be regarded as science fiction, were it not for the mental institutions in the former Soviet Union that were used to "cure" illegal religious believers and other dissidents, and were it not for the fact that officially permitted hostility toward groups of persons with identifiable cultural and religious practices is not a static process, even in a democracy. Such a process grows when economic and political factors create the need for scapegoats, and it feeds on a moral indolence of the general population. The rise of the Third Reich certainly proved that.

Of course, all of that is a kind of worse case scenario. We don't have to go to the logical conclusion of antireligious sentiment to illustrate how inappropriate it is in America. To illustrate that point, all we have to do is look at history.

The overwhelming bulk of the founders who attended the constitutional convention in Philadelphia were church-going believers. They included Presbyterian Hugh Williamson, a former preacher from South Carolina; Roman Catholics such as Daniel Carroll of Maryland; and Quakers John Dickinson of Delaware and Thomas Mimin of Pennsylvania. James Madison, himself had once studied for the ministry.

In fact, Madison studied under Rev. John Witherspoon, a preacher. Witherspoon himself is worthy of study as an influential example of the successful merger of religion and politics. He was a member of the Committee of Correspondence, a member of the New Jersey Senate, a signer of the Declaration of Independence, and ultimately the President of the College of New Jersey, which would later become Princeton University. Respect for the active interplay between those versed in theology and the terrain of political science is an American tradition.

President George Washington, in his farewell address said this: "Reason and experience both forbid us to expect that national morality can prevail in exclusion of religious principle." To our founders, the separation of political and social morality from the context of religious belief would have been unthinkable. Today it is a fact of life. Our failure, as a society, to experience any real sense of conquest over drugs, violence, and the disintegration of many of America's families is the best evidence of the failure of a national moral consensus. To Washington, the explanation would have been clear: reason and experience require that religious principles energize and direct a nation's collective morality. How many more bitter harvests do we need to reap as a nation before we yield to this proposition?

Harvard historian Perry Miller in his book, <u>The Life of the Mind in America,</u> points out that the early religious revivals in the 19th Century were not just aimed at saving souls. That was their primary goal, to be sure, but they were also viewed as a means of transforming and reforming the social community, of correcting evils and promoting the public good.

There was a parallel in Great Britain, where William Wilberforce, applying his theology and appealing to the prevailing religious belief of England devoted his life (and certainly successfully in the end) to rid the United Kingdom of the bane of slavery.

Not only does history teach us the folly of excluding the influence of religion from public policy issues, but the prevailing attitudes of the people of this nation continue to show us how deeply religious we really are.

In the last few years, polls from <u>Time/CNN</u>, <u>Gallup</u>, and <u>Newsweek</u>, and others have consistently shown us a portrait of a nation which is thoroughly religious:

90% of us believe in God

60% believe in the need for a personal experience with God

70-80% of all Protestants, Catholics, and Jews believe that

their church or synagogue had a substantial influence on their morality

82% believe in a literal Heaven and Hell

78% support voluntary Bible reading and prayer in school

73% support prayer at athletic events

and 74% oppose removing references to God in public oaths

The things of the spirit continue to invade an otherwise grudgingly secular society.

Pope John Paul II's book, <u>Crossing the Threshold of Hope</u>, topped the best-seller list, beating even the tell-all book about the life of Nicole Brown Simpson. Gospel rap group D. C. Talk's last album sold an eye-popping 800,000 copies, which is impressive even to secular music stars.

Even scientists are seeing the necessity to reconcile their rationalistic views with their religious faith. Astrophysicists Joel Primack and his wife Nancy, both of the University of California recently told <u>Newsweek</u> how they have come to find, in medieval Jewish texts, a harmony with the idea of an expanding universe, a concept that they were to publish in an issue of <u>Tikkun</u> magazine.

This jarring contrast between our natural orientation toward things sacred and spiritual and the increasing pressure for a religiously sterile, secularized society was aptly illustrated by, of all sources, <u>TIME</u> magazine. Perhaps when even they recognize the inequities of this contrast, the situation has truly become alarming. Here is what they said:

> "In this nation of spiritual paradoxes, it is legal to hang a picture in a public exhibit of a crucifix submerged in urine, or to utter virtually any conceivable blasphemy in a public place; but it is not legal, the federal courts have ruled, to

mention God reverently in a classroom, on a football field, or at a commencement ceremony as part of a public prayer."

Most assuredly, there will come back the answer to this cruel paradox: Yes, perhaps it seems quite unfair, and even somewhat tyrannical, but such are the requirements of "separation of church and state" under our Constitution—alas, were that it would be otherwise! In the next breath, when an Amendment to the Constitution is mentioned, however, the separationists warn us about "tinkering" with our delicate constitutional balance. They want it both ways. The fact is that the separation of religion out of the process of running our nation, our states, and our communities, is seen by some as a positive public good, not just a constitutional necessity. And that philosophy is truly antagonistic to the ideals of religious freedom. Some of our presenters at this symposium will be addressing the legal and constitutional issues regarding the religious liberty issue. And that subject is certainly driven by questions of jurisprudence. But it also goes beyond those questions to the way in which all of our freedoms relate to each other.

Historian Roland Bainton, in his work, <u>The Travail of Religious Liberty</u> makes this point:

> "All freedoms hang together...civil liberties scarcely thrive when religious liberties are discarded, and the reverse is equally true. Beneath them all is a philosophy of liberty, which assumes a measure of variety in human behavior, honors integrity, respects the dignity of man, and seeks to exemplify the compassion of God."

So while it is true that God is not mentioned in the Constitution itself, in effect, it assumes His principles of morality, fairness, and freedom. Perhaps that is why John Adams commented that: "Our Constitution was made for a moral and religious people. It is wholly inadequate for the government of any other." Self-government not only requires vigilance, it also requires virtue. And virtue will only prosper to the extent that we allow our spiritual dimension to have the fullest reign possible, both in our personal lives and our public responsibilities.

It remains, therefore, for us to take up the task of reviving the spiritual lives of Americans, and to call for the fullest degree of freedom for the role of religion in addressing and solving the tough array of national problems that lie in our path. This calling of religion to freedom and action is not going to happen without some sense of the historic moment we face: of the historic unravelling of much of our society's fabric; of the historic problems that we face as a people; of the historic antagonism toward the validity of religion as a source of answers to those problems.

America has faced other historic challenges: the threat of Soviet Communism; the world-wide threat of Nazism; and, of course, the civil war that divided our country and yet helped define freedom at the same time. When President Abraham Lincoln delivered his annual message to Congress on December 1, 1862, he challenged our political system to make good the promise of freedom to an entire population that had been enslaved. His call to the fight for freedom was the same call to which Americans have courageously responded at those other historic times. He said:

> "Fellow citizens, we cannot escape history. We and this administration will be remembered in spite of ourselves. No personal significance can spare one or another of us. The fiery trial through which we pass will light us down, in honor or dishonor, to the last of generations...we...hold the power and bear the responsibility. In giving freedom to the slave, we assure freedom to the free—honorable alike in what we give and what we preserve. We shall nobly save,

or meanly lose the last, best hope of earth."

To the extent that we give full freedom to the exercise, practice, and profession of religious faith, we grant freedom to us all, and we will nobly save the nation that is the last and best hope among the nations of the earth. The alternative, quite simply, is, to quote Mr. Lincoln, to "meanly lose" the future of America. The choice could not be any clearer, and the stakes could not be any higher.

II. ALTERNATIVE VIEWS OF PLURALISM: CHRISTIAN PERSPECTIVES

PLURALISM AS A MATTER OF PRINCIPLE

James W. Skillen

The question of pluralism in the United States has long since become more than a question of simply how best to separate the institutions of church and state. Doing justice to religious diversity remains an urgent matter, and I intend to address it here. Religion amounts to more than participation in church or synagogue. Life outside those obviously religious institutions is not entirely unreligious nor does all of it come under government's direct responsibility. So the question of society's diverse structure ought to come to the fore when we talk about pluralism. How shall we account for and do justice to families, schools, and the media, to life in universities, industries, the professions, and the arts?

Those who give assurances that they will not discriminate against anyone on account of religion do not say very much when they merely affirm their commitment to the separation of church and state. Because if what follows is their insistence that the public square must be kept free of religion and/or that the majority's will should be given free rein everywhere outside churches and synagogues, then the prior "assurances" hold some real dangers. Those assurances presuppose precisely the kind of religiously deep commitment to a sacred/secular dualism, or to a monopolizing majoritarianism, or to both, that cannot possibly do justice to people who do not share the same commitment. The chief political and constitutional disputes about religion today are about whether citizens are free to live according to their convictions outside as well as inside their churches and synagogues. And for many citizens these disputes now center on schooling and family life, not on the freedom to worship.

My argument, then, has to do with two distinct but closely related kinds of pluralism in a politically organized society. It is an argument for pluralism as a matter of principle, not merely as a means of accommodating an unavoidable diversity. It is an argument from justice for the proper treatment of all citizens.

Structural Pluralism

The first of the two pluralisms for which I want to contend is what we might call *structural* pluralism. The intent of the phrase "structural pluralism" is to say that government and public law should do justice to the full range of social competencies or realms of human responsibility—the various institutions, associations, organizations, and human relationships of society. The differentiated character of our society cannot be accounted for by reducing it to free individuals or to a single collectivity. This is due, I would argue, to the fact that this world is God's creation, and the historical diversification of the creation's complexity is neither arbitrary nor fully attributable to individual and social construction.

Political constitutions, for example, which mark off the tasks and limits of government, arose from the recognition that government has its own distinct responsibilities and is not omnicompetent. Other social structures have their own moral integrity and competence. As society differentiates into an ever more complex array of social institutions and organizations, government's task of securing justice entails the recognition and protection of that structural diversity as part of its legal integration of society. Justice for the commonwealth requires just treatment not only of persons as *citizens* but also of all non-governmental institutions and human relationships. A just political order, therefore, will be a complex community characterized, in part, by its principled maintenance of structural pluralism.

Confessional Pluralism

The second kind of pluralism that I affirm as a matter of principle can be called *confessional* pluralism. By means of the First Amendment to the U. S. Constitution, government is obligated to protect the religious freedom of its citizens. This restriction means that the just treatment of citizens requires that government give fair and equitable protection to a variety of religions, not because every religion is presumed to be equally correct or true on theological grounds but because government's competence to establish public justice coupled with its incompetence to define and enforce religious orthodoxy leads to the principle that government should uphold confessional pluralism.

Now the point I especially want to stress here is that religious ways of life (the confessional diversity) express themselves throughout the structural diversity of society. People's religions must not be identified only with their ecclesiastical practices and affiliations. Nor may government assume to itself the right to define as non-religious all things outside churches and synagogues.

Confounding and Ignoring the Two Pluralisms

Unfortunately, too many Americans either confound or ignore the distinction between structural and confessional pluralism. The confounding occurs when religious practices are identified only with the churches and synagogues. The *structural* distinction between two institutions—church and state—is then thought to be a sufficient basis for confessional pluralism if citizens are granted freedom of religion in their churches and synagogues. But religious freedom should not be identified only with the freedom of churches.

Likewise, people often ignore the distinction between structural and confessional pluralism when they overlook the religious convictions and principles that obligate Americans outside as well as inside their churches. If people mistakenly think of the public arena as a single, undifferentiated community of "secular" citizens who, by majority vote, may rule with one will on all things outside churches and synagogues, then every law or Supreme Court ruling will be thought of as having an unrestricted secular authority throughout the public realm. Religious diversity, from this point of view, can be adequately protected in private life—where confessional religion ought to be confined. The public arena is then treated as one big melting pot without structural boundaries or confessional distinctions. This is a grave error and a fundamental violation of religious freedom since it ignores the reality of religion, of competing ways of life, at work in all areas of life.

My contention is that the Constitution does not give government the right to confound religion with, or to confine religion to, institutional churches. Nor does government have the right to pass laws that ignore publicly expressed religion and thereby trample down the distinction between the two pluralisms. Insofar as religions express themselves in organized institutions of worship, confession, theology, and discipline, then naturally a diverse array of churches will appear, and each should receive equal treatment under the law. But, I repeat, religions express themselves beyond the walls of churches. Believers of different stripes may be obligated by their faith to educate their children in distinct ways, to eat different kinds of food, to pursue their occupations with peculiar commitments, and to exercise their responsibilities quite distinctively in a variety of professions such as medicine, law, and even politics. For government to confound confessional and structural

66

pluralism is to restrict religious freedom to churches, synagogues and private conscience—a restriction that actually violates the exercise of religion for many people.

When structural and confessional pluralisms are confounded, the result, almost inevitably, is that people and government ignore the important distinction between the two in public life. If religion is mistakenly thought of as belonging only to churches and synagogues, and if the ideal of a secularized, public melting-pot hides from view the reality of societal differentiation, then it is entirely possible that governments will assume responsibility for education (for example) in a way that overlooks and violates both the structurally distinct identities of families and schools as well as the religious convictions that citizens might wish to express in education.

Doing Justice to Diverse Peoples in One Political Order

If, as I advocate, citizens are given constitutional protection to practice their religions freely (confessional pluralism), then all citizens should be free to conduct family life, schooling, and other social practices (structural pluralism) in ways that are consistent with the obligations of their deepest presuppositions and faiths. One obvious outcome of this argument, for example, is that government should give the same legal and financial support to a diversity of school systems—both those that are obviously religious and those that make no religious claims—as the way to do justice to both structural and confessional pluralism. This also happens to be the only way for government to avoid the establishment of a religion or antireligion.

My argument, which contends both for uncoerced religion and for the recognition of societal differentiation, in no way conflicts with the norm of integrative public justice for a single political community. It simply extends with consistency two principles already enshrined in the Constitution. It seeks, first, to safeguard the religious freedom of citizens, not allowing government to confine religion illegitimately within the institutional limits of church life, and, second, to safeguard the legitimate spheres of responsibility outside government's competence. By insisting on these two elements of pluralism, my argument aims to secure and to strengthen the fundamental pillars of a unifying and integrative civil order—an order qualified by justice for all. In fact, only laws that treat all citizens fairly in their actual social and religious diversity will be able to carry the moral force necessary to bind them together as citizens in a single republic.

PLURALISM: ANOTHER WORD FOR FREEDOM

James M. Dunn

"In the past half-century, American society has become noisily and notoriously pluralistic. This has made Roger Williams more relevant, for he had strong opinions about what government should do about religious pluralism: leave it alone. Turks, Jews, infidels, papists: leave them alone."[1]

These eloquent words of Edwin Gaustad offer a working characterization of pluralism. This specific Christian perspective is one shared by Franklin Littell in his pioneering study, From State Church to Pluralism. Littell concludes, "The situation of religious voluntaryism and pluralism in which the American Protestants now find themselves, understood historically, is a positive good—both theologically and politically."[2]

The challenges to the sort of pluralism spoken of by Gaustad and Littell are many and varied. On the other hand, the popular acceptance of the reality of pluralism, as Robert Booth Fowler puts it, is "the greatest challenge for the New Christian Right."[3]

---

[1] Edwin S. Gaustad, Liberty of Conscience (Grand Rapids: William B. Eerdmans, 1991), p.219.

[2] Franklin H. Littel, From State Church to Pluralism (New York: The Macmillan Company, 1962), p.200.

[3] David Cantor, The Religious Right: The Assault on Tolerance and Pluralism in America (New York: AntiDefamation League, 1994), p.68.

The traditional threats to pluralism are clear. One is triumphalism. This spirit is not academic. I speak from experience. I grew up in a Baptist church in which we were taught to be soul winners. To be a witness to the power of God was not enough. To share our faith lovingly and to depend upon the Holy Spirit to convict of sin and righteousness was not adequate. We had to "draw the net" and we were taught how to do just that. Many, if not most, conservative Christians today have a better understanding of evangelism, but militant, manipulative "outreach programs" are alive and well.

Pardon, if you can, further confession. For a dozen years I directed the social justice programs of the 2.2 million member Baptist General Convention of Texas. With our 5,500 churches scattered through every legislative district of the state, we had to be good stewards of influence. We learned on the state level what many evangelical Christians are only belatedly understanding on the national scene. Since we could not deny the existence of power, we could not but be good stewards of it.

We led crusades that stopped the legalization of gambling in 1968, 1974 and 1978. We made a difference in juvenile justice, prison reform, welfare, pornography and drug laws—heady stuff! We, of course, had to write about it—Politics: a Guide book for Christians was the result. Imagine my chagrin when 15 years later I picked up Newsweek to see Jerry Falwell pictured holding up a copy of it suggesting to all the world where he had learned politics. Pitfalls to avoid as seen from the pit.

Sometimes the triumphalism is so theologically parochial, so evangelistically fueled, and so ethically insensitive that outsiders cannot even imagine its depth and pervasiveness. Excellent illustrations are current attempts to comprehend the anti-Semitism of pro-Israel evangelicals. Of course, it's possible, maybe even nec-

70

essary, to tout the nation Israel without loving Jews, caring about religious freedom or respecting their history or beliefs. For take-over-minded fundamentalists, Jews are but pawns for narrow eschatology and/or prospects for evangelism—hardly candidates for an "I-Thou" relationship.

Less offensive than the "We are #1" attitude but still troubling is the promotion of toleration as the mother's milk of pluralism. Both Christians and Jews fall into this trap. It's easy to do. Toleration is certainly better than intolerance.

Yet, Roger Williams had something when he saw toleration as a "weasel word." It implies a superior and an inferior party, the tolerator and the tolerated. It is concession of men. Freedom is the gift of God. Pluralism is on shaky ground if it rests on mere toleration.

Theologism, the religious parallel to scientism, is a misplaced faith in propositions and sincerely held theological beliefs marketed as the necessary pillars for public policy. Carl F. H. Henry frequently reminds us that "there is no direct route from the Bible to the ballot box."[4] In a way, the phenomenon of which I speak is nothing more than a sort of sophisticated, soft-shelled triumphalism. The notion that the better trained, more theoretical evangelical has a corner on a just and redemptive approach to politics may offer only a difference in degree and not a difference in kind from those who are more overtly theocratic. In fact, timid theocrats may be more dangerous to the voluntarism at the heart of the American experiment than the noisier kind. They are not as easy to spot.

The foundation for freedom that we call pluralism is not without burdens, Brunner's "awful burden of freedom." Princeton professor Clifford Geertz says that "thanks to the deprovincialization

---

[4] Carl F.H. Henry, "Evangelicals Out of the Closet, But Going Nowhere?" Christianity Today, January 4, 1980, p.21.

71

of the world, we're going to be in each others' faces more."[5]

We are already experiencing that syndrome in the tide of multiculturalism that "has raised the consciousness of the academic community, even as it has also raised the contentiousness within that community."[6]

The danger of ethical relativism is frequently linked to pluralism. In fact, the word "pluralism" is used pejoratively by many evangelicals, often as a code word for the absence of absolutes.

The anthropologist Geertz says it well, though in a different context:

> "Understanding what people think doesn't mean you have to think the same thing. You don't just say 'whatever you do is fine,' just saying 'it's their culture' doesn't legitimize everything...I hold democratic values, but I have to recognize that a lot of other people don't hold them. So it doesn't help much to say 'This is the truth.' That doesn't mean I don't believe anything."[7]

Geertz argues that the task is to find a way to keep one's values and identity while living with other values—values you can neither destroy nor approve.

Still another approach to dealing with pluralism in the political context is the adoption of a lowest common denominator sort of civil religion. The religion of the national political conventions sweeps over us like a warm bath. It neuters religion and prostitutes

---

[5] David Berreby, "Clifford Geertz," The New York Times Magazine, April 9, 1995, p.46.

[6] Edwin S. Gaustad, "Barbarians and Memory," Journal of Church and State, Vol. 37, Number 1 (Winter 1995), p.9.

[7] Berreby, Op. Cit., p.47.

politics. Many see God as the national mascot.

The oft cited example of civil religion at its worst is the appeal by President Eisenhower: "Our form of government has no sense unless it is founded in a deeply felt religious faith, and I don't care what it is."[8]

In 1973 Senator Mark Hatfield, whose conscience keeps getting him in trouble, shook up a national prayer breakfast with this comment:

> "If we as leaders appeal to the god of civil religion, our faith is in a small and exclusive deity, a loyal spiritual advisor to power and prestige, a defender of only the American nation, the object of a national folk religion devoid of moral content. But if we pray to the biblical God of justice and righteousness, we fall under God's judgment for calling upon His name, but failing to obey His commands."[9]

So, perils there be plenty in pluralism. What shall we do?

Harry Truman used to say that he hated those "two-handed fellows, who were always saying 'on the one hand, but on the other hand'." Sociologists have given the concept the acronym "otohbotoh." Alas, it cannot be avoided. In fact, an approach employing a frank acceptance of the tensions between the contradictory and the complementary may help maintain integrity and retain humility.

When it comes to Christian citizenship and political participation, there is a need to strike a balance between opposites or counterparts of a common theme: conservatism and liberalism, civil

---

[8] New York Times. Dec. 23, 1952, p.16.

[9] Edwin S. Gaustad, "Religious Liberty: Baptists and Some Fine Distinctions," American Baptist Quarterly, Vol. VI, Number 4, (December 1987), p.244.

obedience and disobedience, order and justice, local and state responsibilities, national and international commitments, and the relationship between church and state. Both parts of the dyad should always be kept under consideration. Conciliation rather than conflict should be the goal. Since tension is inevitable, every effort should be made to make it creative tension. Compromise and accommodation may even lead to or be real reconciliation.

A few illustrations of this sanctified ambivalence come to mind: the tugs between the individual and the institutional aspects of life, the challenge to patience between instant and incremental tactics, and resolution between the tendencies to emphasize the idealistic or the incarnational assaults on a social problem.

Individually, we understand that the pluralism protected by the separation of church and state enhances rather than diminishes personal freedom. Separation of church and state does not mean separation of the believer from citizenship, or separation of God from government, or even separation of politics from religion. The principle does have, however, something significant to do with shaping the proper role of religion in American politics.

When institutions are involved, the separation of church and state is the law of the land, a reality that has been good for religion and good for government. No matter what some latter-day revisionists may say, this distinctive contribution of America to the science of governing is alive and well. Church and state have different constituencies, different purposes, different sources of funding and different methods.

Instant resolution of all problems beckons. Bill Moyers says that the digital clock is a metaphor for American life: we see nothing before or after the present moment. Faithlessness in the power of the truth they proclaim seems to mark the rush to legislate or even amend the United States Constitution on the part of many of the political preachers. They certainly have no corner on that impatience but incrementalism seems wise when we consider tinkering seriously with fundamental freedoms, especially the first freedom.

Sober judgment is advised before we allow government to institute any taxes for religion, tests for theology or laws for prayer. A critical evaluation suggests that political panderers and well-intentioned moralists may be moving in that direction.

John Leland, Baptist evangelist on the Virginia frontier, said: "Experience...has informed us, that the fondness of magistrates to foster Christianity has done it more harm than all the persecutions ever did."[10]

Theologies and theories not rooted in a realistic assessment of the human condition do more harm than good as well. Too often the churches suffer the bankruptcy of disembodied idealism. This is as true of gung ho political activists as of the monkish mystics who practice a strategy of withdrawal.

Reinhold Niebuhr tried to warn of this limit of liberalism in Moral Man and Immoral Society and behold, some of us acted as if he had no glimmer of the truth and others are even yet behaving as if he had told the whole truth.

The alternative to sterile head trips, whether secular or sacred, liberal or conservative, Reformed or Anabaptist, is not "realism." What's that? Rather, the balancing factor to our loftiest political pies-in-the-sky may be a fully fleshed-out attack. An incarnational idealism should call out the best in all people of faith.

Christians facing pluralism need to remember that the church is a divine-human institution. That is not settling for a lower view

---

[10] L.F. Greene, ed., The Writings of the Late Elder John Leland, (New York: G.W. Wood, 1845, reprint, Arno Press, 1970), p.278.

of our corporate expression of faith. The truth be told it is in tune with our highest aspiration—to be like Jesus, of whom it is said in Philippians 2:7, he "emptied himself, taking the form of a slave, being born in human likeness...humbled himself and became obedient to the point of death." How can one argue with that sort of self-giving? What intellectual display can begin to match sacrificial caring for people?

When confronting pluralism we are all called to accept people, understand their beliefs, work together for the common good as we understand it. The best thing government can do for religion is leave it alone. The best thing we can all do for church and state is keep them separate so that neither is caught in the bear hug of the other.

The American way of pluralism has worked well. This nation has the greatest freedom of religion, the least religious conflict, the largest number of people in church/synagogue/temple/mosque every week, the highest percentage of voluntary religious participants, the most missionaries and people-helpers sent out to other countries and the best record of giving in the name of religion of any nation on the face of the earth.

As Senator Kennedy said at Jerry Falwell's Liberty University in 1983, "The foundation of our pluralism is that government will never determine which religion is right, and religion will not put its imprimatur on some politicians while damning others because of their political views."[11]

---

[11] Senator Edward M. Kennedy, Address at Liberty University, Lynchburg, Virginia; October 3, 1983.

III. ALTERNATIVE VIEWS OF PLURALISM: JEWISH PERSPECTIVES

GOD IS NOT A PLURALIST

David Klinghoffer

When Rabbi Rudin and I spoke for the first time, we talked a little about the meaning of the word we were going to discuss. What exactly is "pluralism?" I proposed that we define it as an attitude of tolerance toward diversity—specifically, an attitude of tolerance toward religious difference. Rabbi Rudin said he didn't feel entirely comfortable about the word "tolerance." For him, "pluralism" meant something more like a "celebration" or at least an "acceptance," presumably a cheerful acceptance, of religious difference. Barry Lynn said the same thing when he defined a pluralist society as one that "not just tolerates diversity in religious belief but celebrates it."

This puts me, the speaker placed opposite Rabbi Rudin, in the awkward position of standing up before my fellow Jews to denounce the cheerful acceptance of religious diversity. This is not a position likely to help me win friends and influence people at the Anti-Defamation League.

In fact you don't often hear people saying unkind words about pluralism. Certainly there are antipluralists abroad in the land— haters and bigots of every religious, ethnic, and national description. But it's hard to think of an example of someone who is not a bigot who has nevertheless questioned the wisdom of a cheerful acceptance, a celebration, of religious difference.

About the only example of such a person I can think of is Jay Lefkowitz, a Republican political activist I know, an Orthodox Jew who lives in Washington, D.C., who was quoted recently in The New York Times Magazine. It was in an article about young conservative intellectuals and this young man let drop a casual comment. "Deep down," he said, "I believe a little anti-Semitism is a good thing for the Jews—it reminds us who we are." The reporter scribbled the remark down, and the letters from readers, predictably, poured in. Jews from across the country were outraged that, in a public forum like the New York Times no less, a Jew would endorse anti-Semitism, however "little."

And yet that is a view I would like to reconsider this morning. My Washington friend didn't, of course, mean to endorse the murderous, raging Jew-hatred of Auschwitz and Bergen-Belsen. Nor did he mean to praise the anti-Semitism that brought about the lynching of Leo Franck, nor the riots of 1992 in Crown Heights. Not at all. Let me tell you what kind of "anti-Semitism" he, I think, meant.

In the Wall Street Journal recently a Jewish woman was quoted about an experience her little daughter had at school. It seems the little girl's friends had passed out literature about Jesus and urged the girl to consider the possibility that Jesus is her savior. The mother was outraged, and said this could not be the same America her great-grandparents had fled to from Russia a hundred years ago. The America she loves is a pluralist place, where religious difference is celebrated. It is an America in which little Jewish girls are not approached in public school with pamphlets about Jesus. This is what James Dunn would call "triumphalism."

Consider another newspaper story. It was reported in the Jewish weekly Forward that the Church of Latter Day Saints, the Mormons, had developed a most curious interest in the Jews who had died in the Holocaust. The Mormons have set about to convert them. According to Mormon belief, through prayer, it is possible to convert the dead, if they died as non-Mormons, to Mormonism.

The Mormons say they merely wish to assist the dead of all faiths in reaching communion with God, assuring them a place in the world to come. But Jewish organizations would have none of it. The Mormon practice was denounced as an affront to pluralism, an insult to the memory of six million dead Jews—a failure to celebrate, or at least cheerfully accept, religious difference. Thanks to these protests, and especially to the efforts of an executive vice president of the United Jewish Appeal, the Mormons have reconsidered the practice of converting the Jewish dead.

Is this really a victory? Is a commitment to pluralism really a sign of spiritual health in American Jews and Christians? Let's talk about Jews first.

Here is another instance of anti-Semitism typical of America as it was until quite recently. In 1950, my great uncle Kalman Klinghoffer was an associate professor at Yale Medical School. When the time came when ordinarily he would have been granted tenure, he was not—because, he was told, of the fact that he was a Jew. He was forced to settle for a tenured position at Stanford. Poor guy.

This, for the most part, has been the nature of "anti-Semitism" in modern America: A reluctance on the part of some Christians to fully accept and celebrate the religious differences between themselves and Jews. In his aptly titled book Chutzpah, Alan Dershowitz decries the fact that (at the time he was writing, a few years ago) no Jew served on the Supreme Court. Professor Dershowitz avowed that Jews should not be satisfied until the Chief Justice of the Supreme Court was a Jew.

I don't mind that there has never been a Jewish Chief Justice. I don't mind that my great uncle couldn't get a tenured professorship at Yale. And I'll tell you what else I don't mind: that until a few decades ago, Christian fathers in this country were reluctant to celebrate if their daughters chose to marry a Jew. As Irving Kristol has said, far from hating Jews, American Christians today love us so much they want to marry us.

For any Jew who cares about Judaism, the most troubling thing about pluralism is exactly this. You modern-day Christian Americans kill us with kindness. You invite us to work in your offices at the highest levels, to study in astonishing numbers at your most elite universities, to join your country clubs, to marry your daughters. And you are killing us. Fifty percent of Jews marrying this year will marry non-Jews. In all likelihood, the children produced by those marriages will not be Jews in any meaningful sense. That is only the most obvious and talked about cost inflicted on us by Christian kindness.

Because, whether Alan Dershowitz wants to admit to himself or not, the Jews have been for two thousand years a people in exile. In the year 70 of the common era the Temple in Jerusalem was destroyed, not to be rebuilt, we believe, until the end of days and the time of Messiah. Three times a day in our prayer, the Amidah, we beseech God to gather the exiled Jews of the world, to rebuild Jerusalem "as an eternal structure," and to restore the throne of King David. America is the most comfortable, most tolerant, most pluralistic place of exile we have ever known, but it is still exile. To deny that, to demand that American Jews be made to feel every bit as much at home as their Christian neighbors, is to make nonsense of a cardinal principle of Judaism. Pluralism, to the extent it causes us to forget that our redemption from exile still awaits us, is the opposite of Judaism. The consequences of pluralism are all around us: Jews who have forgotten that they are Jewish.

If pluralism is in some ways the opposite of Judaism, in what relation does it stand to Christianity? There are many other people at this symposium far better qualified than I am to answer that question, but I'd like to offer a few thoughts.

Imagine a Christian father who celebrates when his son tells him he intends to marry a Jewish woman. How serious a Christian could this father really be? A child raised in two religions is almost invariably a child raised, for most practical purposes, in hardly any religion at all: just as children who receive a "bilingual" education usually end up illiterate in two languages.

What about the news stories I mentioned earlier? How serious is the Christian who can be persuaded to avoid mentioning Jesus when he is around Jews, out of fear that he will offend Jews like the woman quoted in the Wall Street Journal? What about a Mormon who believes he can save the souls of dead Jews by offering prayers on their behalf? What does it say about his commitment to a principle of his faith if he desists from seeking to save souls in order to placate the feelings of bureaucrats at the United Jewish Appeal?

Today liberal Jews and Christians alike define anti-Semitism to include not only acts of violence and intimidation, which responsible Christian churches have (at least officially) rejected for centuries, but also any act or instance of speech which presumes that in matters of faith there is truth, and there is untruth. The Christian father who objects when his daughter marries a Jew affirms, whether he knows it or not, that there is such a thing as religious truth, and that he wants his children to marry in accordance with that truth. The same goes for a Jewish parent who objects when his son marries a Christian. The Mormon who prays for the souls of Jewish men and women affirms his faith in the principles of his church—just as the children who pass out literature about Jesus to Jewish children affirm what they see as the truth of their church.

The question of pluralism is crucial because it forces us to confront a most basic choice: is religion about the search for Truth about God, about what God wants from us, or is it not?

Make no mistake: advocates of pluralism are not secularists.

Secularists don't want to hear God mentioned anywhere beyond the door of the church or synagogue—and even that they're not so sure about. Pluralists, on the other hand, are sincere friends of religion, and welcome it when it plays what they believe to be a positive role in public affairs. As they continually remind us, religion was behind the great moral crusades of American history: from the Revolutionary War to the abolition movement, from the Protestant-led temperance movement that resulted in prohibition to the agitation of the 1960s in favor of civil rights. Pluralists earnestly welcome religious advocates of all faiths to the "public square."

In other words, pluralists welcome religion as a useful force for social transformation—and to the extent that the transformation it effects is for the good.

But this raises a final, still more fundamental question: Is religion important because it is useful? Or is religion important because it is true? We are confronted here with the choice between the instrumentalist theory of faith, and the truth theory. Is religion about man, or is it about God?

If religion is about man, if it is man's creation, then we are correct to celebrate religious difference. What right does a Mormon have to tell a Jew his soul is in danger? What right does a Jewish parent have to object to intermarriage, if what is at stake isn't God's will, but rather the true love of a man and a woman? After all, faith is about man, not God. Why not enjoy the differences between Judaism and Christianity, just as we enjoy the differences between English literature and Chinese literature, between Mexican food and Indian food?

"Pluralism" is one of those words that doesn't simply denote an aspect of reality—like "hunger" or "hatred" or "Hillary Clinton." Instead it carries a burden of ideological assumptions—like the expressions "pro-life," "pro-choice," or "homophobia."

Take "homophobia." To say that someone is a "homophobe" assumes a number of things that using a word like "hatred" does not. It assumes, most fundamentally, that there is something profoundly inappropriate about making moral distinctions on the basis of a person's choice in sexual partners. To use the expression "pro-life" makes another assumption: that, in the case of abortion, there is actually a "life" at stake apart from the life of the mother. The assumption carried unconsciously in the breast pocket of "pluralism" is that religion is a creature more of man than of God.

However, if religion is about God, and about Truth, I'm afraid the situation is different. If God cares about the Truth, about what we believe to be the Truth—and that is the assumption of Western religion, whether Jewish or Christian—then we are obliged to act and speak accordingly. Often that makes us uncomfortable, as it should. To be in exile, as we Jews are, is not a comfortable state to be in. Nor is it a pleasant responsibility of Christians to remind us that we are in exile.

But then God didn't put us on earth to be comfortable. Whatever He is, He is not, I think, a pluralist.

A JEWISH PERSPECTIVE ON THE RELIGIOUS RIGHT

A. James Rudin

The first thing that should be said is that the important questions raised by the Religious Right must not become some kind of Jewish-Christian conflict or confrontation. Indeed, I strongly believe the term "religious right" is a more accurate and inclusive definition than the narrower and often used "Christian right."

There are committed Jews and Christians on all sides of this issue, and it is both divisive and even dangerous to view it as an interreligious clash between two faith communities. Rather, the development of the Religious Right, and the many issues it has raised are, at their core, fundamental American issues. What is at stake is determining the future of America as we near the 21st century. And as we debate that future, we need to take exceptional care not to define that debate as a conflict or contest between Jews and Christians. It is not.

However, some polls indicate that the majority of the Religious Right's supporters are white evangelical Protestant Christians. And the overwhelming majority of the Religious Right's national leadership, including such well known personalities as the Rev. Pat Robertson, the President of the Christian Coalition, and Dr. Ralph

Reed, the Coalition's former Executive Director, are in this group.

Until the late 1960s, most Jews in the United States, like many other Americans, tended to underestimate, even denigrate the spiritual attractiveness and potential political power of evangelical Christianity. In the century following the Civil War, or the "war between the states" as it is best known in the American South, that form of Christianity was often perceived as irrational, pre-modern, and benighted.

Although, by definition, all Christians are commanded to be "evangelical," that is, to spread the good news of the Gospel, today the term is usually applied to those Christians who have had a personal, life changing spiritual encounter with God and/or Christ, who believe in the "inerrancy" of the Hebrew Bible and the New Testament, and who actually seek converts to their new found faith through missionary activities.

Despite the profound fervor associated with these three basic standards of evangelical identity, it was widely believed in many quarters that progressive or "liberal Protestantism" would supplant the "old fashioned religion" of the former Confederacy. This belief was best expressed in the play and film, Inherit the Wind, which is a thinly disguised treatment of the famous Scopes "Monkey Trial" that took place in Tennessee during the 1920s.

In real life the attorneys in that case personified more than two conflicting views of evolution. William Jennings Bryan epitomized the "traditionalist" and "backward" view that saw evolution as un-biblical, hence un-godly, while Clarence Darrow represented "enlightenment" and "modernity" in his affirmation of evolution.

But evangelical Christianity was neither supplanted nor replaced by liberal Protestantism. It simply went "underground" for a century. As a Jew growing up in Virginia during the 1940s and 1950s, there was never any doubt in my mind that a broad based theologically conservative Protestantism was alive and well. Indeed, my home town in those years could be accurately called a stronghold of "that old time religion" sprinkled with small pockets of Jews, Roman Catholics, and liberal Protestants.

I distinctly recall the fervent religious faith of many of my classmates in elementary and high school. There were constant reports during Monday morning public school classes of "being saved" the previous Saturday night at a Christian revival meeting. Such conversions were commonplace.

And while there was always a strong deeply anchored conservative evangelical Protestantism in the South, there was not much direct linkage of that faith commitment to the political process. There was a widely expressed belief back then that "politics was not God's business," that politics was a "dirty but necessary" process. What truly mattered was "getting right with God," having a personal religious experience.

Two parallel forces were continually at work: a strong religiously conservative stream and an equally strong conservative political stream, especially after President Franklin Roosevelt was elected to a third term in 1940. It was, as they say, no accident that the devout parents of my classmates repeatedly returned two highly conservative politicians, Harry F. Byrd and Willis Robertson, the father of Pat Robertson, to the U.S. Senate.

But in the late 1970s the two parallel forces met and meshed, forming what we today call the Religious Right. A Southern Baptist minister from Lynchburg, Virginia, Jerry Falwell, and a veteran political conservative activist, Paul Weyrich, were perhaps most responsible for this alliance. Falwell's Moral Majority (a brilliant name since all non-members were by definition members of the "immoral minority") organization was a high profile operation during the 1980 Presidential election.

Falwell attracted those people who believed America and Americans have lost their moral compass. And while non-Religious Right people of faith might also share this diagnosis about America, there is sharp disagreement regarding the kind of medication and treatment the 260,000,000 "patients" require.

The 1980 election revealed that perceived "values" are clearly much more important to Religious Right voters than the actual church membership of political candidates. In that election two of the three major Presidential candidates, President Jimmy Carter and Representative John Anderson, were active members of evangelical churches. Carter, a Southern Baptist from Georgia, proudly reminded voters that he taught Sunday School classes during his years in the White House. The third candidate, Governor Ronald Reagan, was a divorced film star, whose church membership was not a prominent part of his political resume.

Yet Falwell's Moral Majority and millions of other conservative Christians strongly supported the Hollywood movie star, and rejected the pious Carter and Anderson. Values were more important than a candidate's accent or church membership. This critical political fact of life about the Religious Right has not changed since 1980.

By 1988 Pat Robertson, a unique combination of Southern Baptist minister, telecommunications executive, and GOP political activist, felt strong enough to enter the Republican presidential primaries. He was unsuccessful in his efforts, and a religious and political moderate, Vice President George Bush, went on to win both the GOP nomination and the Presidency.

Many voters in 1988 sharply criticized Robertson for "running away" from his professional identity as a member of the clergy. Because of his defeat at the polls, many observers falsely assumed that the movement Robertson embodied was also defeated. But between 1988 and 1992, he established the Christian Coalition, the most active and prominent political group in the large panoply of Religious Right organizations. Perhaps sensing that a defeated presidential candidate like himself could not effectively organize the millions of potential Religious Right voters, Robertson chose a Christian layman thirty years younger than himself, Ralph Reed, to direct the Christian Coalition.

While it was Robertson who actually delivered a major address at the 1992 Republican convention in Houston, it was Reed who did much of the political organizing that resulted in the Christian Coalition's strong influence at that convention. It is estimated that a third of the delegates to Houston were Coalition members.

Some observers express apprehension that the Religious Right seeks to take over one of America's two major political parties, the GOP. There is also concern that if this were to happen, the Republicans might then be labeled "the Party of God," and the Democrats would be the "Secular Humanist" party. This would be a catastrophe for many reasons, especially since the United States has never had the kind of religious political parties that are so familiar in other parts of the world.

The Christian Coalition's basic political agenda is expanding as it attempts to broaden its membership base. In addition to the Coalition's core "family issues" that were incorporated into its 1995 "Contract with the American Family," it also advocates reduced taxes, smaller government, and more direct financial grants to the fifty states—all basic conservative issues. And the Christian Coalition is actively seeking to add Blacks, Roman Catholics, and even Jews to its membership rolls.

The dramatic rise of the Religious Right, and especially the Christian Coalition, has raised some serious questions for the

American Jewish community. While the United States is increasingly a multi-religious, multi-racial, and multi-ethnic nation, groups like the Christian Coalition are often perceived to be advocating an exclusivist America; an America that in the critical arenas of politics and governance would bestow special preference upon its own particular brand of Christianity.

At the same time the Religious Right has created a near public monopoly over the use of such terms as "family values," "traditional morality," and "public righteousness." This is especially unfortunate, and it will take much time and effort before these and other similar terms can again become part of the general discourse in America.

For too long the American Jewish community and like-minded Christian colleagues were either passive or too self-satisfied during the Religious Right's remarkable rise to prominence in the 1970s and 1980s. As a result of this indifference, once valued terms have been taken away, even expropriated by the Religious Right, and the entire political and religious field of discourse has been seriously diminished. Such issues as women's rights, public school curricula, the selection process for choosing library books, creationism vs. evolution, authentic family values, vouchers for parents who send their children to religious or private schools, and other church-state issues will continue to be battlegrounds, and many of those battles will be fought on the Religious Right's terms and turf. By defining the terms and field of political engagement, the Religious Right has achieved a major victory.

Even though several Religious Right leaders have publicly repudiated the continued use of the term "Christian America" to describe our nation, a strong belief remains among many Jews and Christians that such an America is the ultimate goal of the Religious Right, even though this intention is often disguised. The deep suspicion remains that the Religious Right seeks to impose its own particular religious beliefs upon those Americans who may not share them. In addition, the constant call by the Religious Right for a "restoration" of traditional American values is both ambiguous and troubling.

What kind of an earlier America does the Religious Right want to restore? Surely, no one wants to go back to an America when Blacks were slaves, when women could not vote, when children had no legal protection in the workplace. And no one wants to return to an America of anti-Semitic quotas in housing, jobs, and education. And no one wants to return to an America without adequate protection and safeguards for our elderly, our infants, and our disabled.

What is usually meant by the Religious Right's call for a "restoration" is the America that existed before the 1962-63 Supreme Court rulings that made mandated, required prayers and other forms of organized religion in our public schools unconstitutional. Indeed, for many in the Religious Right, those Court rulings represent the "great divide" in American history.

At the time of this writing, we are witnessing an intensified effort to undo those Supreme Court decisions through the adoption of a "Religious Equality Amendment" that would tamper with the Bill of Rights, something that has worked well in the United States for over 200 years. Many American Jews and Christians sense that Religious Right leaders are neither comfortable nor satisfied with the relationship that currently exists in America between religion and state, and they seek to change it by means of a Constitutional Amendment.

I am convinced most Americans strongly believe the guarantees of the First Amendment are sufficient, and they further believe that the First Amendment has insured a robust and voluntary religious life in America; one that is the envy and wonder of the world. One of those precious Constitutional guarantees is that no denomination, no matter its size or influence, can claim it is "America's Religion." There is no officially established "Church of America," and there must never be one.

But I sense a larger canvas than simply the introduction of required prayer during public school hours; a larger canvas than even the adoption of a Constitutional Amendment that would significantly weaken our Bill of Rights for the first time in history.

A much bigger question is being asked: is one particular religious group attempting to gain control of the American political scene, instead of working, as all other religious groups do, within that great mixing bowl we call the American political system? And, of course, it is within that mixing bowl where our laws and policies eventually emerge. But that cannot happen when there are exclusivist claims of divinely inspired political truths.

America is a place where all citizens of whatever religion or of no religion engage equally in the political process. It is where candidates do not invoke divine authority for their various political positions, nor do they await the second coming of Jesus or Armageddon to solve all of our nation's political problems. America is a nation where political opponents are not labelled sinful or un-godly if they disagree with the Religious Right. America is, however, a nation where people of all religions and people of no religion, but citizens all, carry out our unique experiment in democratic self-government.

It must be clearly recognized that the Religious Right is frequently a strong, vigorous supporter of the State of Israel, and many Religious Right leaders express an awareness and understanding of the evil of the Holocaust. Indeed, the general evangelical community is the single largest body of consistent Christian support for the

Jewish State within America.

But despite the Religious Right's strong support of Israel and its public condemnations of the Holocaust, some of the published writings of Religious Right leaders are deeply troubling because they appear to be condoning, even justifying old anti-Semitic canards.

Such anti-Jewish statements and writings undermine national unity and are backward steps in the building of mutual respect and understanding between Jews and Christians. Religious Right leaders could make a significant contribution to the struggle against anti-Semitism by repudiating and eliminating all such negative references in their writings and public speeches.

For its part, the American Jewish Committee will continue to do what it has always done since its founding in 1906: remain true to its basic principles as it seeks appropriate coalition partners, especially like-minded Christians, on issues of mutual interest and agreement. And on some questions, the Religious Right, with its commitment to the safety and security of the State of Israel and its emphasis on the evil of the holocaust, will find the AJC a supportive ally.

But on other important issues the AJC will differ with the Religious Right. Just as there is a plurality of religious expression in America, all protected by the First Amendment, so, too, the host of political views and opinions are all protected. No one group has a monopoly on political truth.

And finally, the American Jewish Committee will never cease to raise the tough questions with the Religious Right just as it has historically done with all other groups on the American scene. To the Religious Right we say: Welcome to the pluralistic political and religious worlds of America. Your views will be heard and evaluated, but they will not carry any special weight simply because you have wrapped them in an exclusivist religious mantle or presented them in the name of God.

A teaching from the Jewish tradition buttresses this position. A certain Rabbi Eliezer was engaged in an intense argument with his colleagues over a particular meaning of the Torah, the Bible. Because his colleagues did not agree with his position, and because he was outvoted, Rabbi Eliezer turned to Heaven for validation and approval. He said: "If the Law agrees with me, despite my colleagues' views, let it be proved from Heaven!"

Sure enough, a divine voice cried out: "Rabbis, why do you dispute and outvote Rabbi Eliezer with whom we agree?" At that moment another sage, Rabbi Joshua, arose and protested: "The Torah was given to us by God, but it is no longer in Heaven. It is now among us here on earth, and we, together, must adjudicate, arbitrate, and legislate. My colleagues, the Torah is no longer in Heaven, and calling upon Heaven will not suffice. Difficult as it may be, we ourselves must make it work here on earth."

So it was then, and so it is with us now.

IV. PRAYER IN THE PUBLIC SCHOOLS

PRAYER AND RELATED MATTERS IN THE PUBLIC SCHOOLS

Samuel Rabinove

We at the American Jewish Committee have always believed that the constitutional principle of separation of church and state provides the most solid foundation for ensuring religious freedom for people of all faiths. Much depends, of course, on how this principle has been interpreted, and that has been at the heart of major controversies over the place of religion in public schools. During the past few decades, the U.S. Supreme Court has addressed a number of cases which involve this issue. More than thirty years ago, as we know, in the landmark cases of *Engel v. Vitale* and *Abington School District v. Schempp,* the Supreme Court ruled that the establishment clause of the First Amendment bars government from either composing prayers or sponsoring prayers for American children to recite.

Is it illegal, as some would have us believe, for children to engage in voluntary prayer in public school? Of course not. There is nothing in any Supreme Court ruling to the contrary. Students can and do pray quietly, in the manner of their own faith, any time the spirit moves them to do so—in the classroom, lunchroom, playground. They can also pray audibly in a group, as long as school routine is not disrupted. Under the Federal Equal Access Act, enacted in 1984, student religious clubs abound, and provide a constitutionally permissible opportunity for devotional Bible reading, as well as group prayer, during non-instructional time. That is truly voluntary prayer. Parents for whom it is important that their own children pray while in public school are, of course, free to guide them accordingly.

What is not legal is for prayer to be imposed on other parents' children, whether other parents may want this or not. The right to engage in voluntary prayer does not include the right to have a captive audience listen—or to coerce other students to participate. In our pluralistic society, public schools are places for students of all faiths—or none.

What about prayers during graduation ceremonies? In the case of *Lee v. Weisman* in 1992, the Supreme Court held that a rabbi's invocation and benediction at a public middle school graduation ceremony violated the establishment clause. "The government involvement with religious activity in this case is pervasive, to the point of creating a state-sponsored and state-directed religious exercise in a public school," said Justice Anthony Kennedy, writing for the majority of five.

Later that same year, however, in the Texas case of *Jones v. Clear Creek Independent School District,* the Fifth Circuit Court of Appeals ruled that a public school district's decision to permit student-initiated and student-delivered non-sectarian, non-proselytizing invocations at high school graduation ceremonies had a secular purpose and a primary effect of solemnization that did not entangle government with or endorse religion, and did not coerce students' participation in religion. In that court's view, therefore, this practice was distinguishable from the facts in *Lee* and did not violate the establishment clause.

More recently, however, the Ninth Circuit Court of Appeals ruled in an Idaho case with very similar facts, *Harris v. Joint School District No. 241,* that such graduation prayers by students did violate the establishment clause, noting that graduation is a school-sponsored event and that attendance is *de facto* mandatory. The Ninth Circuit ruling thus creates a conflict between two Federal appellate courts, making it more likely that at some point the U.S. Supreme Court will attempt to resolve the conflict.

Is a directed moment of silence permissible in public school classrooms? In the case of *Wallace v. Jaffree* in 1985, the Supreme Court held that an Alabama law violated the establishment clause because its *"sole* purpose" was to promote prayer in public schools. Thus, a moment of silence intended as a means of inducing prayer is not permissible. But the Court has never ruled unconstitutional a neutral moment of silence, without such intent, if the purpose were no more than to settle students down, for whatever thoughts they may wish to think, including religious ones, before the start of the school day. If that were all that is sought, however, there is certainly no need to amend the Constitution, or even to pass legislation to achieve this. Any teacher or principal can simply direct it.

On a related religious issue, is it permissible to teach *about* religion in public schools? Public schools, of course, must be neutral with regard to religions. The maintenance and furtherance of religion are the responsibilities of churches, synagogues and homes, not of public schools. While teaching religion to inculcate religion clearly is not permissible in public school curricula, there is nothing unconstitutional in teaching *about* religion *objectively,* including its powerful impact on our civilization. Pertinent references to religion, even to doctrinal differences, whenever intrinsic to the lesson at hand, can and should be included in the teaching of history, social studies, literature, art and music. For example, events such as the Crusades, the Inquisition, the Reformation and the colonization of America, as well as the Holocaust, would be hopelessly distorted if religious motivations were not given proper weight.

Care must be taken, however, to insure that the teacher's religious identity, or absence thereof, does not color his or her instruction. Where discussion of doctrine is not relevant to an understanding of subject matter, the teacher should refer students to home, church or synagogue for interpretations. In sum, from an academic point of view, public schools may educate *about* all religions, but may not favor or disparage any religion.

If teaching *about* religion is permissible in public schools, why not teaching about "creation science" too? In the case of *Edwards v. Aguilllard* in 1987, the Supreme Court struck down a Louisiana law which mandated equal time for the theory of "creation science" whenever Darwinian evolution theory was taught in public school science classes. The Court found that the purpose of the law was not secular but, rather, was to promote a particular religious belief, which violated the establishment clause. "Creation science," although presented as a scientific theory, is really a matter of religious faith, i.e., it happens to coincide with the biblical account of creation as set forth in the Book of Genesis. As a Federal judge commented in an earlier "creation science" case in Arkansas, *McLean v. Arkansas:* " What kind of scientific theory is this that is not subject to revision—ever?" While "creation science" cannot be taught in public school science classes, it may be studied as a religious belief in an elective course in comparative religion at an age-appropriate level. Schools may not refuse to teach the theory of evolution in order to avoid offending religious believers, but students who are offended by such teaching should be excused.

Are religious students permitted to proselytize other students in public schools? A public school, obviously, is neither a house of worship nor a parochial school. Hence, organized proselytizing does not belong in public schools. Parents who enroll their children in public schools for the secular education mandated by the state have a right to expect that their children will not be proselytized away from their own faith and into another which may be anathema to them. This does not mean, of course, that there is anything unlawful if a student invites another to attend church or synagogue or a religious event, or expresses to another particular religious beliefs. But it does mean that no student should be subjected to harassment or coercion by another whose religious convictions are so powerful that he or she feels impelled to thrust such views on one to whom this is unwelcome.

Since public opinion polls find that a majority of Americans do support restoring organized prayer in public school, and since America is a democracy where the majority rules, why shouldn't such prayer in public schools be restored by Constitutional amendment? A *New York Times/CBS* News Poll (December 6-9, 1994), found that 64% of adults polled believe that organized prayer should be permitted in public schools. But when the follow-up question was asked: whether organized prayer is an issue you would like to change the Constitution for, 59% of the respondents said that the Constitution should not be changed for this purpose, while only 29% favored amending the Constitution.

Even if a large majority of Americans were to favor restoring organized school prayer, it should not be forgotten that the Bill of Rights, in general, and the First Amendment, in particular, are anti-majoritarian, i.e., their provisions were intended to protect the rights of minorities, dissenters and heretics by placing certain matters, like religion, outside the reach of transient majorities. Justice Robert Jackson had it exactly right in *West Virginia State Board of Education v. Banzette* (1943), when he said:

> "The very purpose of a Bill of Rights was to withdraw certain subjects from the vicissitudes of political controversy, to place them beyond the reach of majorities and officials and to establish them as legal principles to be applied by the

courts. One's right to life, liberty, and property, to free speech, a free press, freedom of worship and assembly, and other fundamental rights may not be submitted to vote; they depend on the outcome of no elections."

Is it permissible to teach traditional, consensus values in public schools? There is surely nothing unconstitutional in teaching in public schools the core values that are broadly shared by people of all faiths: honesty, decency, sportsmanship, civility, courtesy, self-discipline, love of country, respect and concern for the rights, freedoms and feelings of others. This kind of teaching can reinforce those parents and clergy who are striving to teach the very same values from a God-centered perspective, at home and in religious schools. It can also provide moral guidance for those children who, because they don't receive it at home and don't attend religious school, are not receiving any such guidance. Teaching consensus values effectively would do far more societal good than artificially induced prayer. And, unlike a prayer amendment, it would do no violence to the principle of separation of religion and government, which protects us all.

Is it constitutional for students to express their own private religious beliefs in the classroom? In general, the answer is "yes," but within reasonable limits. Students are free to make religious comments when relevant to a subject being discussed in class. They are also free to give voice to their religious views, when relevant, in the papers they may submit on various topics, or the art they may create. Teachers should grade such work neutrally, as they would any other, irrespective of its religious content. Students do not have the right, however, to turn the classroom into a vehicle for missionary activity.

What about "See You At the Pole" religious observances? There is nothing unconstitutional about students meeting voluntarily at the flagpole for religious observances, when classes are not in session. But school personnel may neither promote nor discourage student participation in such events. While there has been no court decision on the matter, arguably teachers and administrators, because of their official capacities, should not participate in such events because their presence would seem to lend official sanction to them.

All things considered, is there any need, for the first time in our history, to amend the First Amendment to allow organized prayer in public schools? Absolutely not. The First Amendment, which both bars government establishment of religion and government prohibition of the free exercise thereof, is the preeminent safeguard of freedom of conscience for all that has allowed this nation, more than any other, to avoid the tragic religious conflicts that have afflicted people in other lands—and do so even today. In 1785, we were warned by James Madison in his "Memorial and Remonstrance against Religious Assessments," "to take alarm at the first experiment on our liberties." No experiment should be viewed with greater alarm than a proposal to amend, for the very first time, the Bill of Rights, which has served us so well for so long.

PRAYER IN THE PUBLIC SCHOOLS

Craig L. Parshall

Within the wide-angle lens of this symposium's overall theme of the role of religion in politics and society, I have been asked to address the more narrowly focused issue of prayer in the public schools. In order to do that I would like to bring our camera lens down very close to the contours and topography of the decision of the U.S. Supreme Court that spawned this controversy in 1962: the case of *Engel v. Vitale*. And in that regard, like Shakespeare's Mark Anthony, I must be blunt and tell you that I come not to praise Caesar, but to criticize him. That decision was wrong about prayer, which I hope to demonstrate. In fact, if we were to define prayer the way it was defined by the late Rabbi Abraham Heschel, as the act of expanding God's presence where we are, then the Court in the *Engel* case officially rendered God *persona non grata* in the public schools of our nation.

The case concerns the use of a short, non-denominational voluntary prayer at the beginning of the school day in the state of New York. Under the interpretation of the lower courts, participation by the students was purely voluntary and the schools were required to allow exemption, from these activities, of the children of any objecting families, so as to be free from any "embarrassments and pressures."

As a side note, let me say that there are thousands of religious families in America today who would covet one-half of the consideration, regarding the right to exempt their children from instruction that defiles their religion, that dissenting families were provided in New York regarding the right not to hear a prayer being said.

On June 25, 1962, however, a five-justice majority of the Supreme Court ruled in the *Engel* case that voluntary or not, these prayer activities were illegal because they violated the establishment clause of the First Amendment. The religion clause of the First Amendment says: "Congress shall make no law respecting an establishment of religion, nor prohibiting the free exercise thereof." Throughout the decision, the Court addressed the supposed dangers of government composed prayers. Let me say, personally, that I see some public policy problems with school composed prayers led by school officials, but I do not see such prayers, if truly voluntary to be violative of the purposes of the First Amendment. I view the voluntary prayers by students and private citizens, in any setting (including the schools) to be not only constitutional but also wise public policy.

Yet in the *Engel* case the Court performed a judicial sleight-of-hand. After pronouncing that the mere fact that government composes the prayers violates the so-called "wall of separation of church and state" (a poorly chosen metaphor of bad history and worse logic which I will address later) the Court then turns to its own view of history to bolster its conclusion—a view that doesn't match the conclusion when we look at it in slow motion.

The Court makes the astounding (and I believe incorrect) statement that "It is a matter of history that this very practice of establishing government composed prayer for religious services" was one of the reasons for early colonists to leave England for the religious freedom of the colonies. I do not believe any credible view of history would support this. David Ramsey, considered to be one of the greatest early American historians wrote, in The History of the American Revolution, published in 1789, that the early settlers and puritans came out of both a dread of "arbitrary" government power, and the desire to secure religious freedom, among other things. But they did not fear, let alone really care about the fact that England was composing official prayers—what they feared were the official acts of England imposing certain forms of official, required church worship and prohibiting others. That is why, at the very epicenter of the intent behind the religion clauses of the First Amendment was a concern, not with the right to be free from the presence of religion, but the freedom from being compelled to practice or profess a religion at odds with personal conscience.

The Court in *Engel* seems to have recognized this, because they give reference to the Act of Uniformity that was passed in England: an Act which the Court described as "passed to compel all Englishmen to attend those services and to make it a criminal offense to conduct or attend religious gatherings of any other kind." Thus the Court used historical examples of religious persecution in England, based on laws there that required participation in a government established religion to prove that voluntary prayer activities in the schools of New York in 1962 were a threat to religious freedom. This represents an unprecedented leap from logic.

To make matters worse, the Court in *Engel* failed to cite even one Supreme Court decision, or one court case of any kind, to support its conclusion. This fact was admitted by the Court in the next year's 1963 decision in the *Abington School District* case where they banned Bible reading and the Lord's Prayer from public schools. However the Court tried to excuse that omission on the ground that *Engel* was based on "principles...(which were) universally recognized." While I do believe there are such things as self-evident truths (some of them are listed in the Declaration of Independence—most notably that our liberties come from our Divine Creator) I don't believe that banning prayer from schools qualifies as one of them.

But perhaps the *coup d'etat* was the Court's conclusion in the *Engel* case that its decision comported with the intent of the founding fathers. Nothing could be farther from the truth.

Thomas Jefferson, repeatedly emphasized that it was the specter of government using its power to "impose" religion on citizens, to "compel" them against their consciences, using the "coercion" of the state by punishment or loss of civil rights to conform to the state's dictates on religion that posed the real threat to religious liberty; and Jefferson said so in his authorship of the preamble to the "The Statute of Virginia for Religious Freedom" drafted in 1777, and adopted in 1786. Jefferson, founder of the University of Virginia, permitted and endorsed the use of prayer and invocation at the first recorded graduation ceremonies there.

James Madison, during the debates on the Bill of Rights, was recorded as saying that the religion clause of the First Amendment was concerned with the freedom from being "compelled" to worship in any way contrary to the dictates of conscience. As President, in 1813, 1814, and again in 1815 he issued official proclamations for national prayer and thanksgiving to God. And of course, there are countless other examples of other of the founders, like John Adams, in both writings and official governmental acts, expressing similar public accommodation to prayer and religious practice.

Underlying this entire debate on prayer in school, as well the Supreme Court's misunderstanding of the dynamic between church and state (which recently animated its ban on graduation prayer in 1992), is the counterfeit jurisprudential currency known as the "wall of separation of church and state"—a phrase minted by the Court in 1947 almost entirely from one source—a letter written by Jefferson in 1802. The phrase seems obviously used by Jefferson to afford protection to religious practice, but instead, was used by the Supreme Court as a sword against religious practice, thus bringing to fruition the predictions of Justice Potter Stewart (a dissenter in the *Engel* case) that such decisions would cause, not the "realization of state neutrality, but rather...the establishment of a religion of secularism" if carried to a logical extreme.

With only a few exceptions, this stilted concept of religion has dominated the decisions of the Supreme Court and the lower federal courts for 48 years. There is a growing consensus, myself included, that believes that the Court is not likely to repent of its error at any time soon, and that it is time to settle the matter through an Amendment to the U.S. Constitution.

But whether cured by constitutional amendment or otherwise, the prayers of students and other private persons in public settings must not be treated as a kind of constitutional contagion, as if it had to be quarantined and hidden for the public benefit. This is so, because that does two damaging things. First, it violates the principles of equality that Madison declared to be the very basis of all law. Religious speech, including prayer, is treated like the unworthy and illegitimate offspring of free speech—not just a second class citizen, but in fact an illegal alien in the constitutional landscape where almost all other forms of expression (as long as nonreligious) are protected.

Secondly, we create, under this present legal confusion, a culture that suppresses, not only the practice of religion, but the public credibility of spiritual values. We pass more and more laws which presuppose the moral ability of citizens to acknowledge and obey civil authority for the public good, and in the next breadth hold in public contempt the very spiritual source that makes moral conduct possible. Like the laws of physics, logic, and other invariables of the universe, we simply cannot have it both ways.

Jonathan Maxcy, an early American preacher, and later, the president of four prestigious colleges, said it this way: "No government except absolute despotism, can support itself over a people destitute of religion...the American people, therefore, have no way to secure their liberty but by securing their religion."

In an age of exploding information, moral ambiguity, and spiritual uncertainty, this much is clear: if America continues its brazen and official hostility against religious practice, it will not have a prayer.

V. CONCLUSION

FIRST AMENDMENT CONSIDERATIONS AND CONCLUDING REMARKS

Carl H. Esbeck

I intend to divide my remarks into two parts: juridical considerations and prudential matters. First, the juridical or legal considerations.

Juridicial Considerations: As a broad generalization, since the early 1980s the U.S. Supreme Court has been shrinking the scope of the free exercise and establishment clauses. In contrast, the scope of the Court's protection of religious expression under the free speech clause has expanded during this period.

There is a failure to keep abreast of the Court's thinking concerning the First Amendment. Many who should know better apparently think we are still living in an era of "strict separation" of church and state. Those of us at this symposium have a responsibility to not confuse (or to be confused by) matters which are really quite separate and distinct in the law. Allow me to touch upon seven common areas of confusion.

1. **We Must Distinguish Between Government Action and Private Action**

   Only government can violate the First Amendment. Indeed,

that is true of every right in the Bill of Rights. This is what is meant when it is said that our Constitution protects only "negative" rights. The Bill of Rights is a list of things that the government cannot do.

The First Amendment says nothing at all as to what churches and other religious bodies can and cannot do. The First Amendment says nothing at all as to what persons of faith can and cannot do—so long as these individuals are not acting in the capacity of public officials or under color of law.

This is why it is nonsense to say that the First Amendment is a check on religious intolerance from all quarters. It is not. Intolerance is prohibited only when the source is government itself.

2. We Must Distinguish Between Government Speech and Private Speech

This point follows from the first, yet it is constantly being muddled such that it bears separate mention. Justice O'Connor stated the rule clearly in the *Mergens* case: "(T)here is a crucial difference between *government* speech endorsing religion, which the establishment clause forbids, and *private* speech endorsing religion, which the free speech and free exercise clause protect."[1] *Mergens* upheld the Equal Access Act, which allows student religious clubs in public secondary schools.

There is no end to the number of government employees who fail to heed this distinction. The Postmaster General of the U.S. Post Office announced in early April 1995, reversing a policy implemented a year before, that children's posters again could be put up on post office walls at holiday times if a child's poster depicts a religious theme. The post office belatedly recognized that

---

[1] Board of Educ. v. Mergens, 496 U.S. 226 (1990).

the children's displays were private speech not government speech.

Other examples are legion: a child says grace before eating at the public school cafeteria and receives a detention; a child reads the Bible to herself during study hall and is sent home by the teacher; in response to an assignment to create a greeting card for her parents, a child constructs an Easter card, but the work is rejected by the teacher as impermissible religion in public school.

Have public school educators been so propagandized by colleges of education concerning Jefferson's "wall of separation" that they are incapable of making a distinction between a government speaker and a private speaker? This is not a hard concept to grasp: a public school does not endorse all student expression that the school fails to suppress.

These mistakes by public school educators are doing incalculable harm. For when the public learns that a child is punished for saying grace over a cafeteria meal or reading the Bible to herself during study hall, it builds the case for a constitutional amendment to overturn the work of a "godless Supreme Court."

3. We Must Distinguish Between Religious Individuals and Religious Organizations

The command of the establishment clause is addressed to church-state relations. It requires the right ordering of relations between religion and the institutions of organized religion, on the one hand, and the offices of state, on the other hand. By contrast, the First Amendment does not command a separation of individual believers from their government—an impossibility, unless one is prepared either to cleave in half the human heart or to disenfranchise all religious citizens.

One practical outworking of this distinction is in the Supreme Court's cases upholding educational funding programs that are truly parental or student choice. The 1983 case of *Mueller* upheld tuition-tax deductions for all parents of school-age children.[2] Three years later in *Witters,* the Court upheld a vocational scholarship program for disabled students enrolling in programs of higher education.[3] It did not matter that one of the students involved sought to use his scholarship to become a youth pastor. And in *Zobrest,* a deaf student could obtain the assistance of a signer without regard to where he attended high school, including a parochial school.[4]

This is not a sham distinction; it is not form over substance. The rationale for this distinction is two-fold: first, merely enabling private religious choice—where individuals may choose or not choose religion—cannot logically be a governmental establishment of religion. The government is passive, not involved in or directing the choice. Second, the aid is being directed at individuals, not at religious schools, thereby reinforcing the desired separation of church and state.

Numerous familiar programs illustrate the rule: income tax deductions on Schedule A of form 1040 for charitable contributions, including religious contributions; the G.I. Bill; the Federal Guaranteed Student Loan Program; and Federal childcare certificates for low-income parents.

4. We Must Distinguish Between Exemptions and Benefits

The government conferring a direct subsidy or other affirmative benefit on religion or religious organizations is altogether different from government refraining from imposing a burden on religion.

---

[2] Mueller v. Allen, 463 U.S. 388 (1983).

[3] Witters v. Washington Dept. of Servs. for the Blind, 474 U.S. 481 (1986).

[4] Zobrest v. Catalina Foothills Sch. Dist., 509 U.S. 1 (1993).

When imposing regulatory or tax burdens on others, government often refrains from imposing the same burden on religious organizations. This is generally done by writing exemptions into the legislation. For example, property tax laws routinely exempt religious organizations, and nondiscrimination in employment laws typically exempt religious organizations in so far as they want to employ co-religionists. The Supreme Court in the *Walz* and *Amos* cases held that these exemptions do not violate the establishment clause.[5]

The rationale, as Professor Douglas Laycock of the University of Texas has written, is that "The state does not...establish religion by leaving it alone."[6] When government elects to leave religion alone, that is the most elementary recognition of a true separation of church and state.

Let me give you a simple illustration. Suppose Congress raised income taxes on everyone except college professors who, because we employed an effective lobbyist, secured an exemption. In a popular sense of the term, you might say that professors received a tax "subsidy." But in a First Amendment sense, I and other academics were "simply left alone" by Congress while all my fellow citizens had a new "burden" imposed upon them.

Beware of ideologues who try to twist the word "exemption"—which in fact is just the state leaving religion alone—into an affirmative "subsidy" for religion, and hence violative of church-state separation.

---

[5] Walz v. Tax Comm'n, 397 U.S. 664 (1970); Corporation of the Presiding Bishop v. Amos, 483 U.S. 327 (1987).

[6] Douglas Laycock, *Towards a General Theory of the Religion Clauses*, 81 Columbia Law Review 1373, 1416 (1981).

5. We Must Distinguish Between Conduct Required by Good Manners and What the Constitution Requires

Individuals cannot by word or symbolic act be forced to profess a belief contrary to their religion. This was the holding in the rightly famous case of *West Virginia v. Barnett*, which upheld the right of Jehovah's Witnesses attending public schools to refuse to stand and salute the American flag while reciting a pledge of allegiance.[7]

That said, however, there is no First Amendment right not to be exposed to information or ideas that are religiously embarrassing or offensive. The well-known *Mozert* case is illustrative.[8] Fundamentalists Christians in Tennessee sought to be excused from a literature class using a widely distributed textbook. The Sixth Circuit Court of Appeals said that in pluralistic America, virtually everything in a public school's curriculum is going to offend some religious group such that a ruling for the students would render public schooling impossible. The students did not have to believe the message or manifest in any way that they agreed with the material. The mere exposure to unwanted ideas is not protected against by the First Amendment.

This distinction works against others besides Christian fundamentalists. For example, a New York court has held that Jewish students have no right to be excused from the study of Shakespeare's *The Merchant of Venice* and Dickens' *Oliver Twist* because of unflattering characterizations of Jews.[9]

Public school teachers, of course, have broad discretion to

---

[7] West Va. State Bd. of Educ. v. Barnette, 319 U.S. 624 (1943).

[8] Hawkins Pub. Schs. v. Mozert, 827 F. 2d. 1058 (6th Cir. 1987), *cert. denied*, 484 U.S. 1066 (1988).

[9] Rosenberg v. Board of Educ. 92 N.Y.S. 2d 344 (1949).

accommodate the religious practices of their students. Hopefully teachers are sensitive to the religious needs of their students and will accommodate them whenever possible. The point to remember, however, is that such accommodation is a matter of good manners and not a First Amendment right.

6. We Must Distinguish Between Teaching Religion and Teaching About Religion

In early April 1995, the Carnegie Foundation in Princeton, N.J., issued a report that criticized public schools for being so fearful of church-state conflicts that they fail to teach values. The result is student confusion about what behavior and conduct is expected of them. Students used to get these values at home, but no longer is that true for many.

Recently a group of scholars released a study titled *Marriage in America: A Report to the Nation.* As Ellen Goodman of the Boston Globe wrote, it should have been called "Divorce in America." The United States has gone from the most marrying society in the world to one with the most divorces and unwed mothers. This, of course, is why many students are not getting values at home.

Family breakdown is off the topic here, except to say that the First Amendment does not stand in the way of teaching students moral values on which there is wide consensus. The frequent retort is, "Whose values?" But I submit that is easily answered. Despite our society's much heralded pluralism, there is widespread agreement on many virtues: tell the truth, keep your promises, don't steal, respect the person of others, hard work will be rewarded, take responsibility for your conduct, violence is not the way to solve problems, teenage pregnancy is destructive.

Civic virtue and moral self-discipline are essential for the continuance of a free society. We must deny that law can be separated from moral concerns, albeit law and morality are not the same.

7. We Must Distinguish Between a Law Based on General Morality and a Law that is Inherently Religious

A law which merely reflects a moral judgment, shared by some religions, about conduct thought harmful (or beneficial) to society is not a law violative of the establishment clause.

In *Harris v. McRae,* the Supreme Court held that the Hyde Amendment, prohibiting federal funding for abortion, did not violate the establishment clause just because it was supported by citizens and legislators who opposed abortion for religious reasons.[10] Similarly, religious groups have a venerable history of supporting legislation abolishing slavery, enacting civil rights laws, and assisting refugees. It would make no sense to hold all these laws unconstitutional merely because the legislation had heavy backing by religious organizations.

As the Supreme Court said in *Bowen v. Kendrick,* only matters "inherently religious" cannot be codified into law.[11] The modern Court has held that laws concerning matters such as prayer, devotional Bible reading, veneration of the Ten Commandments, and certain symbols that are necessarily religious are prohibited by the establishment clause.

In late March 1995, I received a telephone call from a lawyer in the Chicago area. He represented a Baptist church that had just intervened in a lawsuit. Apparently in Illinois gambling is a matter of local option. A gambling corporation was suing a municipality to have the city remove from an upcoming ballot a referendum proposal to disallow gambling. The referendum was placed on the ballot by citizen petition, and one of the major movers behind the peti-

---

[10] Harris v. McRae, 448 U.S. 297 (1980).

[11] Bowen v. Kendrick, 487 U.S. 589 (1988).

tion drive was the Baptist church. So the suit alleged that the anti-gambling ordinance, if passed, would violate church-state separation. This is sheer nonsense. I am happy to report that the state judge saw it as such and refused to alter the ballot.

Religious people have the same right as everyone else to codify their moral values into law. And they may serve in legislative bodies and evaluate the merits of proposed laws using their moral values as shaped by, among other factors, their religion. As the Eighth Circuit Court of Appeals stated the matter nicely: "We simply do not believe elected officials are required to check at the door whatever religious background (or lack of it) they carry with them before they act on rules that are otherwise unobjectionable under the establishment clause."[12]

To conclude this juridical section of my paper, the First Amendment is not the trump card that will determine very many of the disputes we have over the proper role of religion in politics. At most, the First Amendment lays down a few rules of engagement. Accordingly, in debates over the role of religion in politics, beware of arguments that the First Amendment determines the outcome.

Prudential Matters

1. The Matter of Public-School Prayer

Responsible surveys indicate that 65 to 75% of Americans support public school prayer. The Supreme Court cases prohibiting school prayer, *Engle* and *Schempp,* were decided in 1962 and 1963, respectively.[13] That's a long time ago, so the issue has real staying

---

[12] Clayton *ex rel.* Clayton v. Place, 884 F. 2d 376, 380 (8th Cir. 1989), *cert. denied,* 494 U.S. 1081 (1990).

[13] Engle v. Vitale, 370 U.S. 421 (1962); School Dist. v. Schempp, 374 U.S. 203 (1963).

power. This matter goes far beyond its support by the Christian Right, a mere 15 to 20% of voting adults.

I think school prayer is a surrogate for two larger issues. First, I think the desire for school prayer persists because for some it is a visible signal as to who is in charge. Where this is the case, we have the old Christian triumphalism. This is to be condemned.

Second, school prayer persists because it answers the questions, "Are we a Nation under God?" and "Are human rights God-given?" This matter of public acknowledgement of the nation's dependence on God, and that our legal rights come from God, is far more difficult than intellectuals admit. Academia and many other knowledge centers have gone over to postmodernism, so there is no universal truth. That is not so with the American masses. And there are respectable voices saying that the masses still believe that if the actions of the state cannot be judged by God's standards, then the state is without restraints. And when the jurisprudence of human rights is unhitched from belief in God, then anything goes. If there is no God, then no external, pre-political standard is available to measure right from wrong. You are left with only being able to distinguish legal from illegal. Many will recognize that all that remains is the positive law views of, among others, the fascists.

Every society, however pluralistic it may be and however much it may tolerate divergent religions and political viewpoints, must nevertheless have at its core some set of immutable principles that anchor its institutions and put them under judgment in times of abuse by its leaders. This does not mean that stability requires unanimity. It means only that in any society capable of functioning as one society, there will always be some values that the vast majority accept without question and will defend, regardless of other differences. Throughout America's history, central to the people's credo is that we are a nation under God and fundamental rights are given by this God.

These are weighty matters to put upon the school prayer debate. Nonetheless, it does explain why such a vast majority of Americans polled still support school prayer, for the struggle has come to symbolize a debate about first principles and the meaning of America.

2. The Barry Lynn — Janet Parshall Debate

This exchange was for a popular audience. It was not for the scholars and others attending the second day of this symposium. At times during the debate I had the feeling Lynn and Parshall were reading fund raising letters to the audience. It was political theater, and hence served as an example of much of what is wrong with public discourse concerning religion and politics.

Barry Lynn was strongest when he made two points. First, the country doesn't need a constitutional amendment to correct errors made by public school authorities when they have foolishly censored the private religious speech and practices of public school students. The solution is to educate these school educators by correcting their errors.

Second, like all other section 501(c)(3) tax-exempt organizations, churches may not endorse candidates for political office. This is a fair tradeoff for the advantages that come with tax-exempt status. When the Internal Revenue Service withdraws exempt status from a church for violating this law, it is proper. However, the IRS cannot purposefully target a church because of that church's viewpoint (i.e., being anti-Clinton). In the recent lawsuit brought by the American Center for Law and Justice against the IRS, it will take a trial on the merits to see if IRS officials were properly or improperly motivated.

Janet Parshall was strongest when she made two points. First, Lynn is off-base with his complaint about Christian fundamentalists being "stealth candidates." All candidates for public office withhold some information about themselves. So in that sense, liberals, secularists, atheists, etc., are all stealth candidates. If Christian conservatives must disclose their religious beliefs up front, then so must everyone else disclose their worldview up front. It is quite understandable why Christian fundamentalists keep under wraps their faith when running for office: there is widespread hostility toward them, especially by the popular media.

Second, Parshall correctly challenged Lynn's claim that the codification of teaching sexual abstinence in the schools is violative of the establishment clause. General morality may and often is codified into legislation, even when the moral postulate is shared by some religions. The Supreme Court has turned back such establishment clause challenges in *Harris v. McRae* and *McGowan v. Maryland*.[14]

Although anecdotes can helpfully illustrate a point, both speakers would do well to remember that anecdotes are not proofs.

3. On The Celebration Of Religious Pluralism

Glen Tinder is surely right when he said that religious and moral pluralism is not to be celebrated. There is a lot of loose talk about "rainbow coalitions" and "the rich tapestry of diversity" as we rhapsodize about American pluralism. It's all pollyanish. Dealing with pluralism is hard work, and as a consequence it brings out the worst and best in us. I resist even saying that pluralism should be affirmed. Rather, the first step is that pluralism should be acknowledged and that it presents a formidable challenge. Next, we should roll up our sleeves and be about the hard task of making society work notwithstanding our deepest differences. A good example of making pluralism work, notwithstanding the obstacles,

---

[14] Harris v. McRae; 448 U.S. 297 (1980); McGowen v. Maryland, 366 U.S. 420 (1961).

is the discussion at this symposium throughout the second day.

In making religious pluralism work, I agree with those such as David Klinghoffer who maintain that "thick" religions that strongly resist being diluted, and that seek to convert, or at least vigorously hold their own with children and family, are the ones with staying power. Acculturated religions are so "thinned out" that they will suffer assimilation. Hence, in dialogues, such as at this symposium, "thick" religions should not be pushed away or regarded as intolerant and offensive. Because such religions have staying power, indeed will probably increase in their numbers, it is all the more reason that they be given a seat at the conference table.

4. On Christian Mistakes Concerning Politics

From 1925 up to the mid-to-late 1970s, conservative Christians were uninvolved with politics and public life. That was a mistake. It meant that public matters were abandoned to others.

The question now is: has there been, at times, an overcorrection for this past mistake? I think so.

- There has been violent protest, inflammatory rhetoric (e.g., wartime military metaphors), demonization of the opposition, and a grasping for political power.

- "Means" count as much as the sought-after "end." Within some Christian circles, there has been excessive focus on politics as the means to correct societal problems. Reforming a culture involves more than just changing laws and leaders. Although law and government are important, neither is the primary means of cultural reformation. Moral values are still formed in the heart of each fellow citizen far more by family, community, houses of worship, and schools, than by law and governmental institutions.

127

- Some Christians forgot to seek the common good. Instead, candidates were voted for (or against) on the basis of single issues. Some did not resist the lure of Christian triumphalism or call for the restoration of a supposed golden age of a "Christian nation."

- Some fell under the sway of a politics of fear, a politics of resentment, or a politics that sees Christians as the new victims. Still others love their country while despising the government, especially the national government. This, while seemingly blind to the contradiction.

- Christians should avoid use of language such as "Christian nation" or "Christian America." It is bad history and bad political philosophy. What we have here is more than name calling by liberal secularists, such as "fundies" or "Bible thumpers," as bad as that is.

5. On Jewish — Christian Relations

With the exception of 1933 to 1945, many Christians are unaware of the history of the Jews and the persecution suffered at the hands of Europeans, often acts done in the name of the Church. Christians should become familiar with this history so as to appreciate Jewish sensibilities and fears.

The American Jewish community makes a mistake when it exaggerates the likelihood of persecution. In late 20th century America, the prospect of any church or Christian movement taking over the levers of civil power and turning its engines of coercion against the Jewish community is remote. If the truth be stated, the mind-set of conservative Christian groups is that it is they who are being attacked by the state. We have two groups here, each role-playing the victim—whereas neither is presently being systematically victimized, nor is class persecution even remotely likely.

To be sure, conservative Christians are increasingly experiencing life in a secularized society, and they don't like it. Occasionally school teachers, for example, have been appallingly ignorant of the First Amendment requirements of church-state separation, and have violated Christians' rights. I have spoken with too many liberals who are in denial over these violations of the rights of Christians. Further, I don't criticize Jews for being vigilant, as well as quick to speak when their rights are violated. But prudent vigilance is far short of nursing a persecution complex. It is in their self-interest for Jewish communities to rein in their fears and keep responses in proportion to current realities. Whatever may be the case elsewhere in the world and in times past, in contemporary America Jews are as much "the ruling insiders" as are the mainline (now old line) Protestants.

Conclusion

Just a closing remark about problem solving versus talking about problems. Through my wife, I have learned that there is a masculine and feminine approach to intractable problems such as the interplay between religion and politics and, in particular, relations between American Jews and Christians.

When my wife comes to me and says she wants to discuss a problem, I listen to what she has to say, analyze the matter, and suggest a solution, possibly even two or three alternative solutions. It is at this point that I get an impatient look, and I finally wise up. You see my wife doesn't want my re-framing the issue followed by a list of solutions.

What my wife wants is my empathetic listening to her giving voice to the problem. There is a popular book entitled, You Just Don't Understand: Women and Men in Conversation, which describes this difference between men and women in how they communicate. What the feminine approach calls for is an airing of the problem. The process of active listening can alone render the problem less of a problem. What is needed is not solutions, but being listened to and taken seriously.

The feminine approach to addressing problems is the best a group of Christians and Jews can hope for when it comes to discussing politics and religion. Given these two complex realities, religion and politics, it is unlikely that a final answer, good for all time, will be forthcoming. Rather, we can expect a continuing dialogue, a conversation that will be perpetually ongoing. The question of what constitutes a healthy relationship of religion to politics may never come to a resting place that will not provoke a new rejoinder. But, like the feminine approach to problems, Jews and Christians simply talking together—as in this symposium—can alone cause the problem to be less "problem" and more "possibility."

REFLECTIONS ON CHRISTIANS IN THE POLITICAL PROCESS

Thomas A. Askew

From its founding, the United States of America has been a bold experiment. With its unique blend of republican government, individual rights and diverse populations, in the world's eyes the country appeared controversial and visionary from the start. Even during the nation's initial century, when Anglo-Saxon males and a Protestant ethos dominated governance and culture, *E Pluribus Unum* was not easily maintained. During the 20th century the expanding perimeters of participation for women, minorities, new immigrants and divergent worldviews have encouraged more *Pluribus* than *Unum*. Especially in recent decades the experimental, even fragile, nature of American society has become more evident. The forces of secular modernity along with dramatic demographic, economic and intellectual cultural shifts have sparked heated debates over public policy, individual versus group rights and the future of the social order itself. These debates have transpired at both the national and the local levels, the latter particularly concerned with public school policy. As persons and communities of faith have energetically entered the debates, and organized politically to do so, questions have arisen regarding the proper, or even constitutional, role that "religion" ought to play in public political discourse: hence, the essays and responses contained in this compilation summarizing a Jewish-Christian dialogue held at Gordon College.

It is well to recall that both historically and contemporaneously, self-identified Christians have not consistently agreed on the most appropriate ways to participate in the democratic political process. All have concurred, however, that the First Amendment prohibition on establishing a national religion or state church does not place religiously derived values out-of-bounds in popular public debate. The founding fathers sought to protect voluntary religious choice and diversity; the First Amendment guarantees the "free exercise" of religion. The founders did not purpose to remove the presence of religious beliefs from any impact on political actions, and felt if limited government was to work, religious values had to supply the moral restraints necessary to avoid anarchy. President George Washington specifically made this point in his Farewell Address.

From the earliest days of the Republic, religious people have called upon biblically inspired convictions to bolster their political arguments. The contests over slavery, prohibition, civil rights, the cold war and current issues (e.g. abortion, gay rights, care of the poor, prayer in schools) all contain value overtones that heighten the emotional quotient because foundational issues and commitments are at stake. The nation has become accustomed to the more theologically pluralistic, mainline denominations' involvement in political debates. Similarly, the National Conference of Catholic Bishops often speaks to political, economic and social issues. It is the organizational success of the New Christian Right that highlights the explosiveness generated when positions claiming theological certainty contend in the arena of pluralistic democracy. Yet, as recent court decisions have indicated, the First Amendment includes religious expression as part of the right of free speech. The difficulty arises from the clash between religious convictions, which claim divine sanction and are deeply held, over against the democratic process with its dependence on a multiplicity of views competing to achieve compromise or temporary consensus through

132

the electoral and political process. The tensions are intensified by the decisions of the courts which have introduced controversial social change by expanding the definition of individual constitutional rights, thus bypassing the legislative process itself.

The basic challenge is: How can persons and groups of deep religious faith and convictions cooperate, work or even co-exist with others in society who do not adhere to the same moral or spiritual principles? In recent decades the dilemma has been exacerbated by the revolutions in sexual mores, the roles of women, the decline of traditional families, concepts of free speech and the removal of official religious observances from the public schools. The remainder of this essay briefly summarizes a sampling of diverse approaches Christians have taken toward political engagement. Then, selected suggestions will be offered for responsible Christian political participation.

It should be pointed out, however, that any attempt to generalize on the involvement of Christians in the political process encounters the profound complexities of American Christianity. There simply is no overarching organization, synod, representative body or individual that speaks for all, or even most, American Christians. The spectrum of ecclesiastical polities, theological outlooks and behavioral pieties are extremely varied. Most informed readers are familiar with the historic distinctions between Roman Catholicism and Protestantism. Usually considered Protestant, the Orthodox (e.g. Greek, Russian, Armenian) join with other Protestant bodies that reflect the classical lines of non-Catholic thought and tradition that derive from medieval and early modern times—the Lutheran, Reformed, Anglican, Methodistic or Anabaptist, the latter ardently opposed to any attempts to form a sacral society in which the state seeks to establish a religious commonwealth. Yet, these distinctions do not adequately interpret the contemporary religious scene. Ranging across the ecclesiastical denominational boundaries are contrasts between those who would theologically define themselves as liberal (or in some cases neo-Orthodox) and others who would claim to be theologically orthodox, often termed "conservative." Among those who usually consider themselves theologically conservative are the evangelicals. Not all theological conservatives would consider themselves evangelical, but most evangelicals would see themselves as theological conservatives who hold to the unique authority of Scripture, an emphasis on personal conversion and discipleship, as well as the priority of sharing the gospel and performing good works. The historic evangelical persuasion, reaching back generations with great impact on the religious ethos of most Protestant groups, should not be equated with one stream of 20th century exclusivist and sectarian evangelical piety known as Fundamentalism. The historic evangelical heritage is broad, dynamic and concerned with both personal faith and social justice; the evangelical outlook is as much a mentality, an ardent exercise in intentional religious devotion, as it is a theology. And care should be exercised to not conflate the evangelical outlook with the views of the Religious Right, whose agenda many evangelicals do not support.

In both past and present, Christian believers have fashioned various responses to the political order. Beyond paying taxes and voting, many of the devout have rejected substantive involvement in politics because of its entanglement with worldly affairs and the compromises that accompany the quest for power. Various sects or traditions have been politically inactive except on rare occasions when they are exercised about some special issues such as a gambling casino opening locally. Until recently many evangelical Christians followed this pattern. While some ecclesiastical leaders or councils have officially taken political positions, most self-proclaimed Christians have usually followed an intuitive politics, separating their lives into the sacred and the secular, the religious and the political, the moral and the morally neutral, the private and the public, with little obvious connection. This type of ill-defined dualism does encourage civic participation and maintaining strict religion and state separation. Yet, it too often reflects a minimal concept of religious life that may overlook larger moral and justice issues; also it frequently lacks the deeper theological insights necessary for a cohesive Christian worldview. In marked contrast, a coterie of Christian leaders and organizations advocate restoring America to its so-called original Christian status. For them, America is a "chosen nation" which has a special covenant with God. Other religions can be tolerated but in every possible way, including legislatively, America must be "returned" to its Christian posture. Not willing to claim America ever was, or should be a "Christian nation" in the absolute sense, others advocate a form of "civil religion." Although not distinctly Christian, this "civic faith" would emphasize providential moral laws that must be observed if a nation is to prosper. Adherents from all religions could participate in this generic religion of the Republic. Critics suggest that at worst this approach borders on nationalistic idolatry and at best reduces God to national mascot status. Proponents answer that minimally "civil religion" reminds citizens of a transcendent moral realm beyond human invention and is recognized in the Declaration of Independence which derives human rights from a Creator God. Without much reflection about it, many American Christians have found this "civil religion" approach congenial to their values and a useful common denominator to infuse the national purpose with broad religious meaning.

In contrast, a small but significant group of scholars and laity find the most comprehensive political philosophy based on biblical tradition and history in the concepts of European Christian Democracy. Drawing largely on the political thought and involvement of Continental Protestant Reformed and Roman Catholic believers, this perspective offers carefully delineated Christian views on political power, the state, society and culture in a plural-

135

istic context. Sometimes it is referred to as principled pluralism. Emphasis is placed on empowering and liberating communities of faith to follow their convictions in the various foundational relationships, or mediating institutions, such as family and school in which people live their lives. Such an approach sets aside conventional American political categories (i.e. conservative, liberal, Democrat, Republican) and develops a distinctive Christian political ideology and vocabulary to form new political collaborations by which to work for public justice in a mixed social order. Obviously, such an undertaking explores political paths American Christians have not ordinarily followed, but it is receiving increased attention. In short, there are no easy generalizations to be made about contemporary Christian approaches to political participation. The above merely samples some ways American Christians have engaged the political process, and does not, for instance, even attempt to describe the complex political and social roles the Black and ethnic churches bring to minority communities.

What, then, are some useful guidelines for Christians to observe when entering the political arena? Some are obvious, others more subtle. Most basically, distinctions must be made between the Church and society at large. The Church simply cannot assume that its standards can be imposed on a democratic, pluralistic society. Churches are responsible in first cause to convince and discipline their adherents to follow biblical values before expecting to influence others. Persuasion and positive example are always more effective than coercion and legalism. Whatever rights, rules, and policies are adopted by government must apply to all citizens equally. It is in the Christians' own interest to stand for civil tolerance and the right of all to pursue their own convictions and interest in the public sphere. In this context, however, the right of religious citizens or groups to organize for political influence is not only constitutional, it is desirable. At the same time, in a pluralistic society it is counterproductive for Christians to demand the display of public religious symbols that give semblance of official state sponsorship of a particular faith.

Christians need to differentiate what are clearly biblical imperatives from those values that are primarily cultural, economic or political. To be effective, believers need to understand the distinction between religious and political actions. The Bible is not a political handbook that leads directly to obvious, simple political answers to complex national and international problems. The Scriptures offer general principles that provide insight but not necessarily direct application. Furthermore, realism about human beings should lead to caution, even humility, in assuming one knows the correct biblical interpretation as applied to difficult policy decisions. Even the most sincere believer is a sinner whose understandings are less than precise and who suffers from the ubiquitous human affliction of mixed motives. An openness to new information, fresh insights and a recognition of moral ambiguities are always desirable.

It is entirely in order to present conscientiously one's political positions, but to baptize them as "the" Christian stance on every public question, especially when other earnest believers disagree, is to cheapen the Gospel. At all costs, care must be taken to avoid projecting Christianity as just another lifestyle that is associated with particular ideological political causes or special interest groups. It is one thing for Christians to critique governmental uses of power; it is another to launch a religious competition for power. Churches or religious congregations have more likelihood of influence for good if they avoid partisan loyalty to one political party or set of candidates. Public issues can be addressed or discussed with fairness and the avoidance of partisanship or simplistic sloganeering. The latter always undercut the credibility of any religious group. Intense partisanship and speaking prophetically to the culture cannot be combined.

To be credible, persons and communities of faith must defend or articulate their positions on a broader base of arguments than an appeal to revealed religion or personal beliefs. Worthy advocacy derives from eschewing overstatement and self-aggrandizing language. To avoid misunderstanding and claim the high moral ground, words that smack of triumphalism, self-righteousness and stereotyping of opponents is counterproductive. Clarity of communication, suitable vocabulary and thoroughly researched policy positions should be the goal. Those claiming biblical inspiration for their ethical and political positions must employ the Scriptures consistently. Selected proof-texting is not acceptable. For instance, it is not sufficient to concentrate only on sexual morality. Multiple passages champion God's concern for the poor, the widows and the unempowered. To ignore these is not speaking biblically. Justice for all, not maximum freedom for atomistic individuals, is the constant biblical ideal. As the prophet Micah declared, God demands that we "be fair and just and merciful and walk humbly with our God."

Cooperation with others outside the Church whose interests and values overlap is essential. There is not an absolute antithesis between Christian and all non-Christian thought. Public life is much broader than the process of politics, and individual or organized Christian participation should take care that political enthusiasm and partisanship do not jeopardize effective communication and cooperation with other groups in the larger community.

That America is currently undergoing a cultural and spiritual crisis, few commentators dispute. Distrust and cynicism toward government and public institutions have been building for decades. Overemphasis on individualism and rights is in danger of undermining responsibility to community and the larger justice. Thousands of the religiously committed are concerned and searching for ways to influence positively the directions of both public policy and society. Finding the proper cultural and political role for communities of faith in modern, pluralized societies is not, however, only an American issue. Since 1948 the state of Israel has grappled with the question. Nor has the Islamic world found satisfactory resolution. Despite the presence of anachronistic state churches of former ecclesiastical establishments, in various European countries, spiritual and cultural drift persists. As the forces of modernity continue to challenge traditional religious visions of the good and just life, there will be no simplistic synthesis.

What then is the challenge to the religiously devout? It is to speak prophetically without descending into hateful rhetoric, easy generalizations or scandalous scapegoating. To confront when necessary, but always with generosity and compassion, should be the watchword. And politicalization should be avoided at all costs. If people of faith are to model voluntary communities of vitality, discipline, cooperation and redemption, they must maintain an independent, balanced voice in the public arena. For though they are but pilgrims here on earth, the faithful are instructed to seek the peace and welfare of the city in which they dwell (Jeremiah 29: 5-7).

CONTRIBUTORS

Thomas A. Askew
    Professor and Chair of History
    Associate Director of the East-West Institute of
    International Studies
    Gordon College, Wenham, MA

R. Judson Carlberg
    President, Gordon College, Wenham, MA

James M. Dunn
    Executive Director, Baptist Joint Committee on Public
    Affairs, Washington, DC

Carl H. Esbeck
    Isabelle Wade and Paul C. Lyda Professor of Law
    University of Missouri - Columbia

Harold Heie
    Director, Center for Christian Studies, Gordon College,
    Wenham, MA

David Klinghoffer
    Literary Editor, National Review, New York, NY

Barry W. Lynn
    Executive Director
    Americans United for Separation of Church and State
    Washington, DC

Craig L. Parshall
Constitutional Attorney, Fredericksburg, VA

Janet D. Parshall
Special Assistant to the President
Concerned Women for America, Washington, DC

Samuel Rabinove
Director of Legal Affairs
American Jewish Committee, New York, NY

A. James Rudin
Director of Interreligious Affairs
American Jewish Committee, New York, NY

James W. Skillen
Executive Director, Center for Public Justice,
Washington, DC

Marvin R. Wilson
Harold John Ockenga Professor of Biblical and
Theological Studies
Gordon College, Wenham, MA

Symposium Participants

Felix D. Arroyo
Chair, Boston School Board, Boston, MA

Randall Balmer
Chair, Department of Religion, Barnard College,
Columbia University, New York, NY

Russell K. Bishop
    Stephen Phillips Professor of History, Gordon College,
    Wenham, MA

Dorothy F. Chappell
    Academic Dean and Professor of Biology, Gordon
    College, Wenham, MA

Lori Forman
    Interreligious Program Specialist, American Jewish
    Committee, New York, NY

Stan D. Gaede
    Provost and Professor of Sociology, Gordon College,
    Wenham, MA

William A. Harper
    Professor of Political Studies, Gordon College, Wenham,
    MA

Diane C. Kessler
    Executive Director, Massachusetts Council of Churches,
    Boston, MA

Lawrence D. Lowenthal
    Boston and New England Regional Director, American
    Jewish Committee, Boston, MA

Ronald P. Mahurin
    Associate Professor of Political Studies, Gordon College,
    Wenham, MA

Elaine A. Phillips
  Associate Professor of Biblical and Theological Studies,
  Gordon College, Wenham, MA

Malcolm A. Reid
  Professor and Chair, Department of Philosophy, Gordon
  College, Wenham, MA

Wesley Roberts
  Pastor, Peoples Baptist Church of Boston, President,
  Black Ministerial Alliance, Boston, MA

Jonathan Sarna
  Joseph H. And Belle R. Braun Professor of American
  Jewish History
  Brandeis University, Waltham, MA

Philemon Sevastiades
  Assistant to Ecumenical Officer, Greek Orthodox
  Archdiocese of North and South America
  New York, NY

Timothy R. Sherratt
  Professor of Political Studies, Gordon College, Wenham,
  MA

Glenn Tinder
  Emeritus Professor of Political Science, University of
  Massachusetts, Amherst, MA

Philip Yancey
  Editor at Large, <u>Christianity Today</u>, Evergreen, Colorado

Note: Affiliations as of April 1995